The Art of Living

Sisifos Publishing

Depression - Freedom from medication and misdiagnosis
A Triology - Book I
Psychoanalysis & Psychosynthesis

Translated from Danish to English by Ishan Gupta

3rd edition

ISBN: 978-87-996093-2-1

Print: Libri Plureos GmbH, Friedensallee 273, 22763 Hamborg,
Tyskland

Panagiotis Charbis - Sisifos

DEPRESSION

- Freedom from medication and misdiagnosis

A Trilogy - Book I

Psychoanalysis & Psychosynthesis

Translated from Danish to English by
Ishan Gupta

Published by Sisifos Publishing

THANKS

What I am and what I have, is because of what I learned from my friends when I found myself in difficult situations.

On July 24, 1974 democracy was restored in Greece. In all fairness it must be said that this started a new era. Vengeance made people blind and obsessive. Yesterday's heroes became tomorrow's villains. Freedom can change pride to disappointment and hatred amongst freedom fighters' ranks, not only against junta officers but one another.

They say that time heals all wounds, so ultimately even the junta officers were forgiven. With this forgiveness hate changed into hope and a chapter of life in which I fought for freedom and confronted the junta's regime was closed. A new circle opened then, not as a freedom fighter, but as a therapist.

To my best friend Philip who through his lonely and negative phases taught me the importance of love in depression. To Dr. Evangelia from whom I learned that it is possible to interpret early childhood grief in a positive way. To my dear friend and composer Nikos who taught me how a lonely man can fight and change the environment for the positive. To Vasilis whose metamorphosis from a depressive into a positive, popular and much-loved man showed me how a depressed person can flourish after therapy. To Hristakis who taught me how music can be a catalyst for depressed human psychosynthesis. To all my clients because they have been my teachers. And finally to Marianne without whom I could not have written this book in Danish.

CONTENTS

PROLOGUE

This book is the first in a trilogy about depression. The majority of the book's content was written in 2000. The book explores psychoanalysis, psychosynthesis and therapeutic treatment of depressed people. Since the therapeutic model is a prototype and therefore singular, it was necessary to divide the book into three different sections, in order to help the reader to understand the therapeutic model: first the psyche, then symptoms and finally the therapeutic method (The Sisifos method).

The therapeutic model that this book offers gives excellent results in practice. Furthermore, it is important to note that therapists who achieve success with treating often unsolvable psychological symptoms of depression often assume the role of a master teacher, either consciously or subconsciously.

I hope the reader can forgive any unintentional technical shortcomings or scientific errors that may be in this book - especially in terms of Freud's theories or, more academically oriented psychology, as I have not studied or followed academic psychological education for many years.

The book is intended to be material for those who wish to gain insight into a major mental disorder - depression. The book's main subject is how to diagnose and subsequently treat depression through therapy. The reader should not think that this is an easy job.

From 1990 to 1992, I found myself completely lost in the labyrinth that is the various forms of depressive symptoms, despite the fact that my only goal was to maintain a simple dialogue with clients. Although through different tactics I was trying to reach into the core of this depression, the results were in practice always disheartening. I was disappointed and almost gave up, and for quite a while stayed away from the subject. Suddenly I realized my mistake and began to see depression from a new perspective and took a different approach.

I came to the realization that the Socrates 'Ekmaekftiki Method' (Socratic Method to highlight/conceive people's hidden or unknown inner truth) that I had been using with my clients for two years was not working. I could not even maintain a simple dialogue with them. The reason was that depressed people in the black zone have an inherent and overriding sense of negative self-esteem, which means that their personal contact with the world is almost non-existent. We (therapists) cannot work with their responses because they always respond the same way and with the same negative feelings.

Today I use Plato's 'shared approach', and this provides positive results. I can not only build trust and get in touch with my clients, but continue with this method throughout dialogue therapy.

An illustrative example:

The client narrates his story - he has experienced so much pain and cries constantly. The therapist begins by acknowledging the client's pain and suffering, but explains that the client is still alive and therefore things are positive (for example, that the client has a strong body and has not suffered misfortune like a heart attack or cancer). The therapist is changing in other words, the client's negative view of finding the positive in situation (that he or she, despite pain and suffering is in good health) and shows the client how to do the same. In this way a connection and dialogue therapy can begin.

In the world of philosophy life begins from scratch or naught as opposed to theology, where the world begins with God. If transferred to therapy, it means that with Plato's Partition method we do not encourage the depressed client's ego, as opposed to Socrates' midwife method where the client has no ego. In the sharing method, we take the opposite approach and develop the client from 'zero' in a positive direction.

This form of therapy dialogue (Plato's Diaratiki method) between therapist and client will be described in detail later in the book, a method with excellent results that leads to a client's ultimate liberation.

In therapy I also use, in parallel with the sharing method, Aristotle's 'confinement method'. I had very positive results with this from 1992 to 2000. As for symptoms other than depression, after the construction of a relationship between the therapist and client, the clients begin to cooperate and their resistance to the therapist takes a passive rather than conflictive or competitive form.
Therapy for depressed people broadened my horizons and changed many of the ideas I had about depression. For example, it is believed that depression is a general condition experienced by many people periodically in their lives. However, I am beginning to understand that depression is a symptom that has some fundamental characteristics that are common to everyone in the world.

So, I choose to split depression into three different categories. The form of depression that occurs early in childhood, I call endogenous or major depression. The second category is really two other symptoms that are related to depression, but certainly not depression, namely - melancholy and martyrdom. The third category is a "depression phase" (really the same as the second category - melancholy) stemming from other symptoms like substance addiction, self-abuse and anxiety. In this context self abuse can mean anything ranging from self inflicted physical pain to bulimia.

The three categories of depression are:

1) Endogenous or major depressive disorder (true depression)
2) Melancholy and martyrdom
3) Depressive phases (stemming from addictions, self-abuse and anxiety)

This first book contains examples of all three categories of depression, so the reader can truly understand a condition that is fundamentally and widely misunderstood. The book is about how we as therapists should respond to our clients and how to separate and identify the three different categories of depression - to which we as therapists must respond and manage differently.

Today, more than 18 years after creating the 'Sisifos method', I still enjoy the same success with clients who suffer from depression. Reading this book will not help you become a specialist on depression. If you do not already have psychological insights you may read this in a literal sense without understanding much. The reason for this is that almost every page contains intense information and perspectives on depression. You will naturally and rapidly feel overwhelmed, even though the book is written in simple and understandable language. In other words, it is not the language or concepts that make it heavy reading, but rather the theme itself - depression and related therapy.

It will be helpful to read the book in chapters – for example start with just the the first topic – psychoanalysis of depressive persons. If you understand this chapter fully, go on to the next. If not, you will understand when you continue reading why it would have been best to stop. You will not understand Sisifos' therapeutic method, if you do not understand the first chapter on psychoanalysis itself.

Enjoy.

THE PSYCHE

Psyche comes from the Greek word 'Psyki' ('psyche' in English). According to Greek mythology, envious of the beauty of a mortal girl named Psyche, Venus asks her son Cupid (Eros to the Greeks) to use his golden arrows while Psyche sleeps, so that when she awakes, Venus (Aphrodite to the Greeks) can place a vile creature in front of her eyes to fall in love with. However Cupid takes pity on Psyche, for she was born too beautiful for her own safety. But before he can scratch her shoulder with the arrow, she awakens and looks right into his eyes, despite his invisibility and he falls deeply in love with her. He cannot continue his mission and this enrages Venus, who places a curse on Psyche that keeps her from meeting a suitable husband. This upsets Cupid greatly, and he decides that as long as the curse stays on Psyche, he will no longer shoot arrows, which will cause Venus' temple to fall.

After months of no one falling in love, marrying, or mating, the Earth starts to grow old, which causes concern to Venus, for nobody praises her for Cupid's actions. Finally, she gives in to Cupid's demands to be with Psyche and everything goes back to the way it should be. People again fall in love and marry, animals far and wide mate, and the Earth begins to look young once more.

But no one still desires Psyche as a wife, Psyche's parents consult an oracle, which tells them to leave Psyche on the nearest mountain, for her beauty is so great that she is not meant for (mortal) man. But Zephyrus, the west wind, carries Psyche away, to a fair valley and a magnificent palace. Cupid visits her every night to sleep with her, but demands that she never light any lamps, since he does not want her to know who he is until the time is right.

Cupid allows Zephyrus to take Psyche back to her sisters but warns that Psyche should not listen to any argument that she should try to discover his true form. Her two jealous sisters tell Psyche, then pregnant with Cupid's child, that rumor is that her lover's true form is a great and terrible serpent would devour her and her unborn child when the time came for it to be fed. They urge Psyche to conceal a knife and oil lamp in the bedchamber and slay him. Psyche sadly follows their advice and recognizes the god Cupid himself. But a drop of oil falls from her lamp onto Cupid's shoulder, wakes him and he flies away.

Psyche goes searching for her lover and finds a temple to Venus and enters it. In order to get to Cupid, Psyche must accomplish some tasks set by Venus. She orders Psyche to separate all the grains in a large basket of mixed kinds before nightfall. An ant takes pity on Psyche, and with its ant companions, separates the grains for her.

Venus is outraged and tells her to go to a field where golden sheep graze and to retrieve some golden wool. A river-god helps Psyche and suggests she pick the wool that sticks to the branches and bark of the trees. Venus next asks for water flowing from a cleft that is impossible for a mortal to attain and is also guarded by great serpents. This time an eagle performs the task for Psyche.

Venus, furious at Psyche's survival, claims that the stress has caused her to lose some of her beauty. Psyche is to go to the Underworld and ask the queen of the Underworld, Proserpina (Persephone to the Greeks), to place a bit of her beauty in a box. This time Psyche is helped by a three-headed dog who guides her to the Underworld.

However, once Psyche has left the Underworld, she decides to open the box and take a little bit of the beauty for herself. Instead an infernal sleep arises from the box and overcomes her. Cupid (Eros), who had forgiven Psyche, flies to her, wipes the sleep from her face, puts it back in the box, and sends her back on her way. Then Cupid flies to Mount Olympus and begs Jupiter (Zeus) to aid them. Jupiter calls a full and formal council of the gods and declares that it is his will that Cupid marry Psyche. Jupiter then has Psyche fetched to Mount Olympus, and gives her a drink made from ambrosia, granting her immortality. Psyche and Cupid become one and the same.

Pythagoras, the father of mathematics, has subsequently defined the psyche as the white butterfly that flies out of a body when people die. Phoenix, as said to rise from the ash of the dead, has also been seen as a symbol of the psyche.

From Greek mythology, it is clear that many psychological observations come from the story of Psyche. Many of these will be elaborated upon in the next chapter on psycho-synthesis. However, I will stress here, the story of Psyche so beautifully describes that if a person loves another deeply, he or she is often willing to go to the end of the world to find their love. In a few words: when you're in love, you feel immortal. For love changes the daily routine of life into indescribable joy and happiness, people in love are filled with light and energy when communicating with authentic world and thus feel immortal. Therefore, we could also that it is the Psyche that shines the rays of love upon humanity.

What I just described is only one of the many psyche characteristics - love and love emotions - but there are others as well. Psyche symbolizes, according to Greek mythology, inner strength – the kind that can make you fearless in the face of death if that is what will bring you to your love.

Another important characteristic of the human psyche is freedom. The paradox of this is that when people lack freedom, for example when in governance by tyranny or dictatorship, when they protect their country and people from an external threat, when their social values are threatened, psyche characteristics become apparent. Soldiers at war are a good example – with a willing smile, they accept death as a possible fate because that may be the price of fighting for freedom.

A very strong example is Gandhi, who by 1919 was leading the opposition against British colonial rule in India. Gandhi, using only his psyche as a weapon stood up against the British government as a one man army, and won. He walked along the Indian coast to gather salt, which the British had monopolized, and finally had two million people join his crusade. Together they managed to push the British out of India, and Gandhi's desire for freedom won over the British Empire. So the second important characteristic of psyche, besides love, is thus freedom - the inner freedom that gives people so much power that they feel immortal.

A third characteristic of the psyche – creativity – is particularly evident during the period of total democracy in Greece. During the golden century of Athens, Pericles (Perikles to the Greeks), a friend of Socrates, was a leading statesmen and general. Pericles was the leader of the Athenian alliance, and as a way of support to the alliance, he spent money to invite some of the greatest poets, philosophers and artists of the time to Athens. As a result, the year 400 BC was the epic pinnacle of a cultural explosion in Athens, started in around 600 BC by the Ionian philosophers Pythagoras, Hieraklit and Thalis Milisios.

Pericles' golden period is the only of its kind in history and the cultural resurgence experienced is unparalleled till today. Besides this surge of philosophy, there was also in this period a major artistic emergence. The temple and miracle known as Parthenon (Acropolis) remains a unique example. So a third, clear characteristic of the psyche is creativity.

Creativity, that I believe is expressed in the form of philosophy, art and poetry, are the three basic components to building new roads in human history. Love and creativity lift a man up and give him personal liberation, which is why we can say that the psyche is a trinity of freedom, love and creativity.

All three characteristics of the human psyche can in theory be experienced after the 18th year in one's life. This brings to question how the human psyche is during and before the age of 18 years. Is it the same from person to person? Do children have an ego or are they totally dependent on their parents? While playing, how does a two-year boy choose between the following things: a dollhouse, a hairbrush, a car or a train? And what would a girl choose? If the boy chooses car or train, how does he play with them? Does he play peacefully or destroy them - and if so, why? What role does the father play in a child's development between the age of four and five years? If children see their father as a God, why do they do this? How do children interact with one another at school (and with society) in the play break (aged seven to ten years) and why? Why do children between the ages of 14 to 15 years rebel against their parents, even though both parents shower them with constant love?

Since all these questions demonstrate different kinds or forms of psyche, it is necessary to define the concept further. Psyche is that which gives form to the human body. It is the channel that builds and creates a person's personality. Personality is a certain behavior, which includes the individual's posture, movement and language, and this behavior is different from person to person. In other words, individuals display some specific characteristics, which we call psycho-synthesis. For example, a two to three year old child's psycho-synthesis is as fundamentally different from that of a 7, 15, 25 or 35 year old man's, as is man and woman's psyche so complete different.

PSYCHOSYNTHESIS

A psyche is the result of conscious and unconscious personal experiences. The unconscious takes shape and form through community ethics and morals as well as through parents' upbringing and relationship during childhood. The conscious experience takes shape when a child is struggling to find place in society's hierarchy (in the neighborhood, at school and in society at large). Conscious experiences can be grouped into five different categories:

1. Environment
2. Family relationships
3. Honor
4. Career
5. Personal failings

1. Environment

All people from the Mediterranean, in part due to the warm weather, express their feelings and opinions loudly and clearly accompanied by strong body language. They spend a lot of time outdoors, taking part in long discussions - often while they are walking or sitting in a coffee shop. In colder climates, as in the north, people express their opinions succinctly and often without feeling, they are always on the move and in a hurry. People in the north "eat" their words when they speak because they want to communicate quickly and without embellishment. So, while people from the Mediterranean often talk using grand gestures and rich language with much color, compared to the north where people often only speak with just their mouths and not with the body.

2. Family Relationships

The type of family form often decides this part of the conscious, namely matriarchy (social organization with the mother as the head) or patriarchy (with the father as head). An example of this is once again Mediterranean people, especially men, who discuss their views and spend much of their lives at the Agora (marketplace). However, it is not actually men in charge here, as it objectively appears, but women entirely. For example in 2003 the EU decided it needed to send sociologists and psychologists to Italy in order to make mothers-in-law aware of the boundaries of marriage and stop them interfering in their sons and daughters lives.

In conflicts between a man and his wife where a mother-in-law is also involved, men often take their mother's side, a pattern that can quickly result in divorce. In a country like Italy this can be disastrous, as most of the population is Catholic and therefore can only marry once. The same pattern also exists in Greece, where mothers can often cross all boundaries to interfere in their children's relationships and marriage. However, most people are Greek Orthodox and can marry up to three times so divorce does not have the same (relatively) disastrous results.

In the north the patriarchal system is common - the father is the provider of the family. This is reflected in the language as well, for example; the word 'gift' in Danish has a dual meaning – it means both marriage and poison. From nature, we know that men are polygamous, so they are reluctant to marry. So the word for marriage subconsciously reflects a man's thoughts on the matter as well – it is poison for him. Another example of how deeply ingrained the patriarchal system is in language and everyday life is apparent - Danes call all French people Frenchmen, even if they are female. It is clear that the men are in charge. In a patriarchy we can expect a well-organized society, scientific reasoning and a well accepted democratic system (the Olaf Palme socialist model).

Matriarchal societies are quite the opposite - undemocratic and/or corrupt (Italy under Mussolini in 1922, Spain under Franco in 1936, Greece under Metaxas in 1936 and the Papadopoulos Junta in 1967). However, in these communities it is feelings rather than logic that takes shape, where passion, drama and love are the cornerstones of everyday life.

In the two kinds of communities I talked about earlier (people from the Mediterranean and the north) men and women still function in their natural gender roles. For example, in a matriarchal society a woman first takes care of her husband's basic needs through sex and maintaining herself for him. Once that's taken care off she then sends him off to work so he can bring home the money for her and their family. This means that the woman in the matriarchal model maintains the relationship, performing and organizing. Women have the power and control the finances but also play the traditional role defined for a woman. As I mentioned earlier, in a patriarchal society the men come first. If there are children involved then the woman must fulfill her duties first as a mother and then as a wife - love for the children and sex for the man.

In late modern society, from the 1980's onwards, we can observe a clear paradoxical phenomenon, which is that natural roles have been completely reversed and this confuses us. In order to understand this phenomenon we can go back to what the Algerians and in earlier times philosopher Albert Camus alluded to - that Spartacus' revolution would make past slaves the new leaders and Romans the new slaves. This is opposed to what all Marxists believe – that all people should be socialists. We can draw a comparison to late modern society where women are increasingly masculine and men feminine. This phenomenon started in the 1970's with the feminist revolution when the women pushed the man out of the proverbial 'Agora' (marketplace) and put themselves in the masculine role. I call this phenomenon the 'Spartacus' effect.

Another apparent phenomenon is that men are spending more time at home, often playing the role of housewife. This new form of social system is called 'metroktoni' (in Greek 'meter' being mother and 'toni' being murder) – essentially meaning destroying the natural balance (mother nature). Women lose their caring, mother role for they work long hours and are as focused on their careers as men whilst their children spend time in day care centers. This leads to a tremendous sense of guilt for not being able to express love through time spent with the child. Consequently, women become increasingly aggressive towards their men for not being able to participate equally in the maintenance of family life and the home.

For example, a typical young mother today is stressed; she leaves work to go to the kindergarten to pick up the children so she can hurry home to cook. The evening will not bring any real quality time with the children, whom she first rushes home and then sends to their room so she can do the laundry, prepare dinner and then help with homework. Naturally, women are good at handling several things at once: watching the children, cooking and talking on the phone with a friend at the same time. This is unlike men who can at best do one thing at a time. Most of a woman's guilt comes from being away from home (after the child's first year), which means that she expects that the man should be able to handle as many tasks as herself. Soon, a 'marital war' starts because the man cannot handle this.

3. Honor

Honor is essential in order to shape society. In a patriarchal system, honor means getting an education and then serving the community. In a matriarchal system, honor is to discover the truth and meaning of life, everyone has an opinion in relation to philosophy and politics. Therefore, they struggle to find out what is right and what is true, and that is why they lack a holistic view of their country as a nation, because they are constantly struggling to find a common truth. For example honor for a Greek man is to be constantly involved in politics, because otherwise he will known as puppet or slave to others. Not slave in the literal sense of the word, but in the sense that he is a dormant part of the community and should just stay home.

4. Work and career

A person's profession and career will define his body language and manner of speaking. A doctor's posture and language, for example, is very different from that of a craftsman. Even within the healthcare community a surgeon and a general practitioner speak a very different language. A surgeon is very clinical in thinking and grave in his tone while a general practitioner is friendly and welcoming. However, pride comes before profession, since it is possible that a craftsman's pride is greater than a surgeon, or a soldier who protects and respects his family or his country more than a scholar. The scholar perhaps gets his honor only by virtue of his job title, and really does nothing substantial for his community.

5. Personal failings

When a person is able to interpret his personal shortcomings and use them in a constructive manner to develop himself, he goes on armed with experiences that help him face fears and maintain a balance. For example, take the case of a 30 year old man facing a crisis in life. He expects moral support from his best friend, but for some reason the friend just turns his back on him. The man then gets help from a third person, who he now believes has "rescued" him. After the crisis passes the man is unable to accept that his friend did not support through a hard time but life needs to go on. A person who now understands that his true friends are those who help in a time of need has seen the objective reality (that his friend was not there for him). If he is unable to accept the new objective reality and continues being aggressive, sad or depressed that his friend did not help him and let him down, he will develop a symptom.

So let us now see how people react to a symptom. So far we have seen that people have their own psychosynthesis in five different categories, affected by different factors such as community, environment, job or family. But when people have a symptom these factors disappear, which is why they react in a certain way regardless of the society they find themselves in, be it a patriarchy, matriarchy or 'metroktoni'. For example, a drug addict reacts in certain ways regardless of whether he is a Dane, American or Ethiopian, or if he was drug addict in the eighties or is one today.

Let's start by talking about psycho synthesis before the 18th year. When children try to find solutions to their problems they seek parental help and start to communicate more deeply with the parents. Up until the 15th year children idolize their parents and their ego is completely dependent on their parents. But a child's ego is different from its parents - a child's ego is problematic because children lack the basic logic to draw conclusions. At this age the child believes that it knows the objective reality, but this is in fact a wish or fantasy. It is because the child idolizes the parents, trying to imitate everything the parents do. But in this process, which in practice is an effort to express opinions, feelings and instincts, the child will make many mistakes.

For example, a 14-15 year old boy has so much dynamism and energy that he cannot even imagine that he makes mistakes. In his world he only reacts correctly. He doubts all other opinions, but not his own, and can therefore react illogically. This is also why boys at this age often find themselves in dangerous situations. In their world death does not exist, which why they often engage in foolhardy escapades in an attempt to show parents and society how strong and fearless they are. In a group of boys drinking beer together, one would gladly demonstrate to the other that he can drink 20 beers for every one beer that the others drink – a completely irrational and over the top suggestion.

Another example is a boy who, driven by basic biological instincts (sexual desire) is very sure of himself, thinks he can easily conquer the opposite sex. On the one hand he feels he can have sex with any girl he desires but in reality will freeze with fear if he even has to ask a girl for the time. The boy understands that his own desire is different from reality (objective reality). When the boy discusses his problem with other boys, he discovers that all his friends have these problems and that reality is not what he imagined - in this example that girls' psychosynthesis is different and girls don't just have sex with boys on a whim. If the boy has developed correctly thus far he will accept that girls are more mature and confident than boys. At this age, boys are often beaten by other boys in front of girls to impress them and are often enemies without cause, only to realize that they need nothing but their own qualities and strength to conquer the opposite sex. Egos can fluctuate wildly in children at this age because both girls and boys are constantly 'up and down' – it is the transition from their own imagination to objective reality. Conflicts and errors are therefore natural. The real problem develops though, if they cannot socialize normally and are unable express personal mistakes and failures to friends, but instead choose to keep their struggles to themselves. In this case they will, rather than have a natural 'problematic' ego, develop a 'Plasma' ego which later evolves into a symptom.

The term 'Plasma' ego comes from the Greek word 'plasma', which means a living organism without a face or body (I usually use the example of jellyfish: an unruly lot, just floating around without form). In people it is reflected as a symptom where a child will try to hide or protect the parents and constantly second-guess parental behavior. The failing here is a lack of love and care from parents, thus explaining the child's guilt (the child has not developed a sense of logic yet) and its eternal struggle (inability) to separate its own mistakes from those of the parents. We therefore refer to these clients' egos as 'Plasmatic' because they project their parents' failings as their own and are thus unable to understand them ergo use them for personal development. Clients with this symptom interpret normal errors as large, personal disasters and are unable to own up to their mistakes. In other words it means that people with this symptom live in their own fantasy world and have problems with socialization and relationships.

When a symptom surfaces and starts to 'bloom' it always displays seven characteristics. For example, the seven characteristics of alcoholics are:
1) Being aggressive
2) Speaking in monosyllables
3) Being a verbal revolutionary - talk about changing society, but not in practice
4) Being accusatory and suspicious
5) Cowardice
6) Seeking escape and building fleeting fantasies through alcohol
7) Protecting the parents and condoning their mistakes

These characteristics usually surface as a symptom between the age of 14-16 and are the consequences of the childhood. The symptom arises from the one fundamental characteristic in the 'Effect' phase (age 9-12) which later explodes into the seven characteristics in the 'Symptom' phase.

For example, an alcoholic often takes on the victim-of-society role - "Look what they have done to me", complaining about the unfairness of society that there is no escaping from. They will go as far as to show off bruises and blood (from beatings as a result of provoking other people). This is the fundamental characteristic of the alcoholic.

We can call the different characteristics of a symptom psychosynthesis. Our job as a (clinical) therapist is to eliminate these characteristics in order to free our clients from their symptoms. Compared to symptoms such as abuse, eating disorders, anxiety, neurosis and narcissism – excluding depression and melancholy though - we work with our clients through three different phases. In this book though, we focus on depression and melancholy.

With depression and melancholy, five phases are required. The fundamental difference when we work with depressive people is that their symptom occurs already at five years of age (not in early life) - so there really is no 'effect' phase (age 9-12) at all but a full-blown symptom itself.

Instead of feeling joy or disappointment as other children, depressed children are fascinated at an early age by 'Thanatos' (Greek for death), something Freud acknowledges as well. That is also why it is so difficult to work with depression because the therapist has to deal with the 'Thanatos' feelings first.

Instead of the three positive characteristics usually seen in the psyche - freedom, love and creativity - in depressed people we see confusion, disorientation and self-inflicted torture. Depressed children feel confused because they lack life instincts, so they do not have the internal need to communicate with other children through play. The depressed child withdraws and feels irresolute and perplexed because he does not know how to deal with the natural hierarchy formation that takes place between children as they build up their ego. The child also finds it difficult to establish a normal dialogue with other children. Subsequently, the child does not manage to create commonplace symbols and idols such as God, a father figure or a favorite football team. Children are heavily influenced by other children's opinions, naturally leading them to build up their idols to look up to (support) God, a football team, their neighborhood (for example a posh neighborhood vs. the ghetto) or family. The depressed child is the epitome of a total failure and that, together with the lack of symbols, is the driving force behind the eternal quest for acceptance amongst the other children. They will accept or agree with almost anything said or done by other children.

For instance, a boy accepts and agrees with the five different opinions of five other boys. He hears that one boy supports Manchester United and says he does too. But he also just heard the four other boys say they support other football clubs, Real Madrid, Barcelona, Inter and Roma respectively. The boy's intention is to make friends by listening and agreeing with all the other boys, but instead he will get the opposite reaction from all of them. If he would just express his own personal opinion that his favorite team is say, Roma, he would at least belong to the group of Roma fans, who would be on his side in the boys' hierarchy.

Or a girl just trying to agree and fit in with the other girls – in this case by copying what the other girls wear, their commonly used phrases or body language - thinks this is the way to get the other girls to like her. But again she will experience the opposite - she makes the other girls furious that she imitates them and they turn hostile towards her.

Both the girl and boy will be provoked into an endless cycle of isolation and passivity by the other children. For example, at some point the other boys will start saying things like, 'Hey idiot, where is Manchester - in Italy or Greece?!' or 'who do you support now, Rome or Barcelona?' The girls will say, 'Look here, I just bought this dress on the internet. You should probably get the same, ha-ha'. The very basis of a depressed child's relationship with other children is spending every moment thinking about ways to agree and connect with other children's issues. Mornings, before coming to school, are spent thinking who they will sit next to at lunch and how they'll respond when the other children tease them. If an entire day passes without incident the child can breathe a sigh of relief when it's time to go home, but only after enduring an entire day of stress. But already that same evening before the child is even in bed, there are already thoughts about the next day and the thousand new questions it could bring. In a few words; the isolation the child has now built for itself with the other children's issues simply creates a vicious circle that the child cannot get out of. The child needs to express his anxiety about the other children and get a response from a true friend. Something like, 'I am scared of responding to the others when they ask me questions in the morning' to which a friend could respond with some encouragement, 'Why don't you just tell them off so they just keep their mouth shut and go away'. If your child hears this from a buddy, he or she can go to school the next day without fear and confusion, but only one concern - how to muster the strength to be able to stave off the teasing children.

The lack of dialogue and normal contact with other children has devastating consequences for a child's mental world. They do not have the courage to tell other children that they shouldn't tease them anymore or that they do not like to play football, even though playing football will help them fit in (because all the other children play football). When these children suffer from depression in adulthood (where it really becomes apparent), they are generally unable to express opposing views. For example, if discussing the terrorist attack in the U.S. on September 11, 2001, depressed people would express regret and sadness. As a therapist one would ask, 'Do you feel aggression towards the terrorists since they are responsible for this act?' The depressed client mutters, 'Well, I do not know, for the terrorists can also be good people.' The therapist clarifies,

'Yes, I do not know either if they are generally good or bad people, but in this situation where they fly into buildings and cause so much death – are they really good or bad people?' The client replies, 'Uh, no, no, no, I do not know, the only thing I know is that I am very sorry.'

Depressed people destroy their logic completely at times by thinking that they are always wrong. They live in confinement and isolation, and often build up a fantasy world where communication with the outside world frequently takes place through the arts (most depressed people think they are artists and paint the world as they experience it, namely as small children). But unfortunately opening this fantasy 'art resort' is not a way to socialize in the real world, which is why they often have disorders such as hypochondria or manic episodes.

The result of years of subjugation and isolation means that beyond the psychological pain, many times the physical pain of the depression can result in paranoia and in extreme cases, suicide. For now we stop talking about psychosynthesis for depression, for we need to go back and explore the reasons why a child cannot build idols and symbols. A question is also at what specific age this submission begins? We will find these answers and explanations when we discuss depressive characteristics in later chapters.

SYMPTOMS

The word psychology is composed of two Greek words - 'Psyki' and 'Logos'. The Greek word 'Logos' refers to an objective, acceptable truth as we know it from the basic scientific principle of stipulating a hypothesis and then proving it to be true. Sigmund Freud talked a lot about the psyche and described the unconscious world as beyond the control of human logic. To explain the psyche Freud used the principle or truth about the Oedipus complex (which for Freud was the objective truth), that occurs when both parents have a good relationship with each other and raise their children well.

When a child is faced with a lack of 'logos' (eg. when parents are lost to divorce, death etc.) or a problematic 'logos' (eg. parental abuse or violent behavior), the child will experience trauma. When a child often lacks care from the mother of limits from the father then the trauma takes over and completely blocks the child's development. The child then begins to builds a plasma ego, trying to protect, idolize or demonize one or both of the parents. During the plasma ego period the child may develop a general anxiety disorder, and to escape the pain, flee the unconscious signs of its symptom.

One symptom is a certain behavior that will cause a person to commit the same mistakes repeatedly. This error will create an imbalance in the person's instincts, emotions and logic, so the person will not know how to avoid failure. This person has not had normal experiences and is thus incapable of deducing what is naturally correct. For example; when a boy sees his father only scolding a passive mother, who is unable to defend herself, the child is fully aware that his father is behaving incorrectly. But what the boy really requires is the image of his father speaking with respect to his mother and apologizing, or the mother offering a plausible explanation for her husband's reaction. If not, as an adult the boy will behave the same way as his father and treat his girlfriend the same way.

Symptoms provide the child fleeting moments of paradise and occur as the third and final part of the tripartite mechanism:

'Cause - Effect - Symptom'

The causes take place in the form of events or circumstances (behavior of parents or missing/violent parents) between the age of 0-9 years. The effects surface as a fundamental characteristic between the age of 9-12 years. And finally, the characteristics explode into a full blown symptom by the age of 14-16. Up until now however, psychologists have failed to identify the causes of any symptom, not even the most simple (agoraphobia, claustrophobia or arachnophobia). And because they are unable to diagnose the cause or symptom it becomes impossible to make practice effective therapy. This is a bitter truth and hard to swallow.

As an example we can take a young, troublesome child who has been expelled from school and displays strong narcotic addiction tendencies It is difficult to accurately tell which symptom this child will develop. So we must wait until the symptom (drug addiction, marijuana abuse or alcoholism) appears, which it does between the age of 14-16 years, and then it will be possible to provide therapy. But if we turn our attention to the 9-12 year period (the effect phase) and it seems like the child provokes other children to beat him, then this is a characteristic which will most certainly lead to an alcoholic symptom.

For example, a stubborn, domineering father and passive mother, can in effect cause a general anxiety disorder between the age of 9-12, because the boy cannot distinguish between right or wrong (for example when parents quarrel). The boy loves his mother and dislikes the father for treating her badly. But the boy also loves his father because his father is strong and takes command, in contrast to the passive mother. On the one hand he doubts the sincerity of his parents love, because they ignore him, instead of expressing their feelings directly. On the other hand, he is inwardly well aware that his parents love him, but he has simply not experienced it in practice. Therefore, he unconsciously provokes his friends to beat him so he can find out if his father will react and protect him. As a part of the provocation, he suggests to his father that he change schools. If the father satisfies his son's wishes and moves him to another school, the boy will develop alcoholism between the age of 14-16. The characteristics of alcoholism will allow him to escape from the generalized anxiety disorder and anti-social behavior that he has developed. Similarly, a child who is in effect mid-way between being passive and trying to protect a friend (when there is fight instigated by the boy himself), but gets beaten while trying to do so, will start smoking marijuana between the age of 14-16.

In other words we can draw from many different examples to see that children can have a fundamental characteristic that later evolves into a specific symptom. As described earlier, a child who provokes others and responds with a 'pitiable sacrifice' (the basic characteristic) cannot develop any other symptom except alcoholism. In the second example, the child protecting his friend and is beaten by the other children in the process is 'passive and defeatist' (the basic character traits), cannot develop any other symptom except marijuana abuse. A third category of characteristics is creating hostage or blackmail situations for friends. For example, a boy who has developed these characteristics comes across a few boys smoking marijuana; he will then threaten to tell the other boys' parents or their teacher about the incident, unless he gets some of the 'goods'. He may even make friends with a much older boy who he will seek protection from and use to threaten the other boys. This boy will later become an addict himself. More precisely, he will first experiment with alcohol and then marijuana, eventually developing an addiction.

From the basic traits during the 'effect period', we can see what kind of symptoms the child will develop. Thus, the logical conclusion is that we cannot forecast symptoms or give therapy for something that is wrong because it is based on a philosophical fallacy. Although we do not know the cause of a problem, we can in effect forecast a symptom and provide therapy for it. If readers want to know how I found all these basic features, the answer is simple: from the therapeutic process itself. After 20 years of working with all forms of abuse, I have noticed that even after removing the symptoms of addicts they are not completely free, but that their abuse is replaced by a new symptom, namely life anxiety. These people, most often male alcoholics, find themselves a problematic partner (with periodic or paranoid anxiety) to complain to (the anxious or paranoid partner dare not leave home so they can constantly play the role of a second father or mother).

When a drug user completes therapy, he often sees himself as a guru and makes other addicts, hostages to their addiction, listen to his story. He does this even though he has been drug free for 10-20 years. He will probably not have a family but can get a job, and when he finally comes into a little money, he holds on to it as long as he can (the trait of a drug addict – trying not to spend money on anything except drugs) and therefore maintains the guru-ego. The former marijuana user can hold on to the job, but he not start a family, because he knows (or believes) that at the sign of first conflict his partner will give up and divorce him (if he has chosen a partner who also plays the second parent role). Former alcoholics need weak partners who play the role a daughter, unlike former marijuana addicts who need to get a mother who can take care of them and control them using money (marijuana addicts are notoriously tight-fisted, almost physically unable to part with money).

On the basis of these examples and through therapy we can observe that even when a client's symptom and its seven derived characteristics are removed, the fundamental characteristics continue to live in the form of life anxiety. It is evident that therapists go as deep as surgeons to find a clients' inner truth. This is necessary if we are to deliver real therapy, so we can accurately understand and explain our clients' reactions.

DEPRESSION - DEEP MELANCHOLY

Like most words in the psychology world, the word melancholy also stems from the Greek language. The word is composed of the Greek words 'Melan' and 'Koli', meaning black and bile respectively. This description is consistent with being afflicted by melancholy, when the world becomes dark and obscure - without a way out and without hope for survival; In other words a negation of life and the world. Lonely people are often poets, artists, philosophers, writers or generally people who are seeking to discover the meaning of life and life's big questions. They all suffer from melancholy at a certain stage in their lives. At this stage they are not able to follow the rhythm of life, but instead withdraw, isolating themselves from the outside world and losing desire and interest in life. Melancholy also affects people who are unable to handle the vacuum that is created after the death of a close circle of friends, people who are separated from their partners or suddenly lose their jobs, and people who have been victims of (or implicated in) unjust situations without the strength to stand up to them. In a few cases it may affect people who have a history of schizophrenia in the immediate family, for example parents or grandparents.

The first known time the phenomenon of melancholy appears in history is in Homer's Iliad from 1200 BC. During the Trojan War, Achilles, the immortal king of Mermedones, is affected by melancholy thrice. The first time is when Achilles feels unfairly treated by the megalomaniac Agamemnon, King of Acheon - Agamemnon steals Achilles' spoils from Vrisiida. The second time is when Agememnon breaks his promise of a marriage between his daughter Eufigenia and Achilles. The third and worst time Achilles is struck by melancholy is when his cousin and best friend, Patroclus, is killed by the great warrior Hector of Troy. In this last case, Achilles expresses pain by anointing his face and body with ashes, tearing his hair out and then isolating himself in his tent for 40 days without food.

Melancholy has from that first time till today, been a phenomenon that occurs in every life story with hardly any change in meaning. However, it has evolved in line with adopted industrialism and the emergence of modern society and has been assigned two new meanings:

1. The word melancholy is used in daily life to describe a loss. For example, each autumn, when summer is over (and lost) we experience melancholy. This is a part of man's natural cycle that follows the changing seasons: every spring we are born again, we enjoy ourselves and are free throughout the summer, experience the melancholy of autumn and stay that way in the cold and dark days of winter.

2. Secondly, we now also experience melancholy if one realizes that he has committed his entire life thus far to materialism.

Melancholy is thus a natural part of the human being. But can melancholy today still be considered a mental illness? And if so, how serious is it? If under great pressure in periods, is it not a natural, human reaction to feel down? How should we as human beings react in these situations? Should we pretend to be happy and blindly commit ourselves to the normal manner? No. Melancholy is a natural, human reaction when we are under a lot of psychological pressure.

This kind of melancholy should not be ignored, but as I said, considered a natural, human reaction. What we must pay real attention to is deep melancholy, also known as depression. Depression is, compared to melancholy, not periodic but constant grief. People with depression experience, apart from melancholia, a pain in the left side of their body which slowly spreads to the rest of the body. This painful sensation can be likened to the feeling of pneumonia throughout the body, with as much physical pain. Therefore, depression often leads to such helplessness and despair that suicide can be the only redemption.

The brevity of depression as a disease is apparent from a study conducted in 1996 by Statistics Denmark. It was found that 200,000 people suffered from depression, which was equivalent to five percent of the entire Danish population at the time. Moreover, the study showed that one third of the population aged 18 years and older will experience an episode of depression in some form and need psychiatric and psychological treatment. The duration of such an episode will last anywhere from six to 24 months and up to 70% will suffer a new episode of depression within two years of recovering from the first. Some people can suffer up to ten episodes of depression during their lives. Ten percent of those suffering from severe depression commit suicide. 60% of all suicides in Denmark are committed by people with depression (1200 persons each year). A small proportion of depressed people, who suffer greatly from anxiety and stress, die each year from heart attacks and many experts today say that this figure has more than doubled.

FEATURES OF A DEPRESSIVE EPISODE

The fundamental characteristics of depression are timid and submissive behavior and a mood of apathy and monotony, which means that the depressed do not have the ability to see the shades of society - in other words they experience living in a grey and colorless world. Often this feeling of a grey world after a long period of deep sadness and disappointment in people is reflected in a feeling of emptiness. For example, the loss of a loved one, with whom the depressed has had a complicated relationship, is a triggering factor. This leaves the person feeling alone and with the inability to organize life or see any hope on the horizon. There is a sense of emptiness and this renders the person incapable of 'receiving' any feelings from the outside world. This is called the grey zone. The grey zone occurs before a period known as the black zone. The black zone is total isolation from the outside world in a period that lasts from 30 days to 6 months - a period filled with the worst kind of pain, as previously mentioned, an experience which causes actual pneumonia-like pain throughout the body. Sometimes people who experience this even come down with a very high fever. During the fever the person may have the extreme experience of vacillating between intense body temperatures. The pain is so strong that it causes temporary paralysis. The afflicted are unable to move out of the house, carry out simple chores and see other people, engage in simple tasks like watching television or reading the newspaper, and generally avoid daylight altogether. For some the pain is so strong, especially in the mornings and evenings, that they lose patience and commit suicide in order to be free from their suffering.

However, for most after the black zone comes once again the grey zone or apathy zone. None of the specialists and experts today can understand the constant pain that their clients have described to them, and the depressed cannot truly describe the pain either. Depressed people find that nobody, not even family and close friends understand the suffering that they have been through. So they decide to distance themselves from others, for example; they may sit in a gathering without speaking or moving at all. This however is only the external picture for the outside world. Confusion prevails inside – this person can only express his or conflicting feelings through irony, cynicism, sarcasm or aggression. For example, the person would never say, 'I am grateful and feeling so comfortable around these people because they understand my pain and experiences." This person has a constant phobia and guilty complex. They believe that life is just punishing them. The combination of self inflicted punishment and guilt allows the individual to isolate himself into the black or grey zone.

Guilt haunts the depressed; they move slowly in short steps and talk in a monotonous and low tone, almost to themselves, because they cannot handle normal dialogue. The face has no expression, and in response to questions they answer in monosyllables. The responses themselves come after a long time and are out of context. 95% cannot communicate in a dialogue for more than five minutes. This is the Achilles heel of psychology. How does one make therapy for the depressed when they cannot communicate and participate in dialogue? Guilt in depressed people is so strong and fundamental (near manic) that it cannot be changed by other people.

Let us take the case of a depressed woman, 42 years old, who feels guilty about her father's illness and pending surgery - a simple, routine surgery for the removal of kidney stones. After surgery the father is apparently well, but not from the depressed woman's perspective. She is (manic) convinced that her father suffers from cancer and will die of the disease, which he is keeping a secret from her. She feels guilt over her father's supposed disease (cancer) because she, years ago was in disagreement with her father over her choice of husband. She married this man despite his father's disapproval and had two children with him. The relationship between daughter and father improved but only superficially over the years. As I mentioned earlier she feels fundamentally at fault - as the oldest of three siblings, her two brothers and she have chose to go their own ways in life which meant opposing their tyrannical father. The moment her father takes ill her guilt peaks. She feels responsible and guilty for his father's (fatal) disease to such an extent that many times she comes close to committing suicide (manic reaction). This is in spite of the doctors, as well as his father, telling her that he is healthy and does not have cancer. For her these ate useless words. Only she knows the truth about her father's cancer and therefore she must be punished severely.

Guilt and self-inflicted punishment take on a fantasy role of epic proportions in her world. She takes examples from her childhood, where she did not listen to her father, so he had been disappointed in her and therefore she must be punished. He has in other words been disappointed with her so many times that finally he developed cancer. The reality is that her father was a tyrant and never gave her any attention or time. She is convinced that she has been a bad child and this is why her father has not listened to or spent time with her. In other words she frees her tyrannical father and punishes herself with guilt. The guilt is so strong that the only thing she thinks about is the future when God will just punish her with death, so she doesn't destroy other people in the same way that she has her father.

OTHER CHARACTERISTICS OF DEPRESSION

Depression manifests itself as guilt in childhood, usually when the child is 4-5 years old. To understand the child's world though, we must begin at the 2-3 year period. At this age the child thinks, as the Greek philosopher Aristotle says, only in pictures. When a child, for example, loses sight of his mother he begins crying, because for the child this means losing the mother forever - even if the mother only goes into the kitchen or garden. The ego in the first years of a child's life depends completely on the mother, who must cope with the child's anxiety and transform it into love. At 2-3 years the child's ego naturally opposes the parents and is reflected in the child's constant 'no' to everything. At 3-4 years boys build up a special ego by defying monsters (toys or action figures), not their parents. Boys aged 3-4 years like playing with monsters - not because they love the monsters, but to fight against them. The difference between boys and girls, even though both are afraid of the dark and monsters, is that girls like playing with dolls – they love the picture of waiting for the prince on the white horse who will come and liberate them from the evil witch. Both boys and girls have a phobia of monsters and evil as part of their fantasy world. Therefore children aged 2-4 years have an essential need for a father. The mother's care is necessary, but the father's love with limits, boundaries and information about the world through play is very important. Children have nightmares where a losing battle may be fought against a monster. Therefore, at 4-5 years they need the father's protection. This is the first time the child places the father in the role of God, rescuing it from witches and monsters. Therefore, in the period when a child has nightmares, the father should be with the child in the room until he or she falls asleep. This means in the child's fantasy world, the father protects it against evil and represents God. In the same way the father going to work everyday is also as symbolic to the child - my father goes out into the world everyday to fight monsters and comes home in the evening as a winner and protector. The father represents, in other words, God.

If the father does not give attention to the child and protect it, the child automatically feels evil (like the monster) or that it has done something wrong. This is a child's brain at the age of 4-5 - my father does not love me so I am a bad person or I must have done something wrong. This means that the child places the father in a different kind of God role - not a God who loves, but a God who punishes. There are two kinds of religious people: those who believe in God as a loving God who forgives and consequently follow his bidding of love and forgiveness themselves too; and the second category, those who follow God's rules because they are afraid that he would punish them and send them to hell. Instead of love, punishment and a place in hell are the drivers of life. They follow God's rules because they fear God's punishment. So when a child sees his father tired, aggressive and disgusted, the child automatically puts the father in the role of the punitive God and feels that it has done something wrong. If the child experiences his father as a God who loves then it will develop intellectually, be happy, social and feel safe (if it commits an error, the father/God will protect). This can be seen very clearly in a child's instinctive love for animals, especially lambs or chicken. Children sympathize with small animals if they are injured, but they cannot understand that these are the same animals they eat. Therefore, I propose never to let small children watch a chicken or a lamb being slaughtered (only from 12 years of age onwards can they can cope with this). If it happens, they will have the worst shock of their lives. It is essential that a child at this age to have an explanation for his father's reactions towards the mother in order to grow up free from guilt. If the mother does not express her love then the child will take on 100 percent of the burden and lays the foundation for depression: all stemming from guilt.

At this age the child cannot reach conclusions itself. For example, the child cannot naturally work out things like: 1) my father loves me, 2) but he also loves my mother, his friends and job. Therefore, the child cannot conclude natural outcomes like 3) my father not giving me attention does not mean that he does not love me, but simply that he is preoccupied with something else, or, my father loves me, but he just does not express his feelings. If the mother does not explain the father's actions to the child, coupled with the father's preoccupations, the child will begin to feel alone and lost in the world. The child thinks that the parents do not give it attention because it is a bad child.

The protagonist of this theory (Sisifos method) is not the mother, as most psychologists today believe, but the father. We can see how depression occurs in the following combinations of mother and father roles, where his father is missing (in his role as God):

1) The weak father - dominant mother combination, both have ordinary jobs: The father is conflict shy and cannot express personal opinions. He leaves his obligations to the mother. The mother plays a dual role as both mother and father, thus making her aggressive and constantly scolding the father. She does not get the necessary support from the father and must take on the father role. This means the child is terribly confused, since it cannot conceive the weak father as God. Since the child is unable to accept that the father cannot be God because he is weak, the child blames itself. And if the mother is aggressive not only towards the father, but also her child, the child will feel even more guilt.
2) Dominant and aggressive father – anxious and weak mother combination, the father may work periodically and the mother has a steady job: The father may be a drug addict, psychotic, very self-centered, narcissistic or megalomaniac. The child will not develop normally if the father is unjust towards the mother or child, and generally without respect and love towards other people – because he cannot be conceived as God. The child feels, as described earlier, guilty (its feeling are akin to Socrates' saying - if God is unjust or numb, we cannot call him God). This is particularly true for girls; they cannot cope with a very aggressive and vociferous father. They automatically take on a protective role, and often become traumatized.

Losing a mother is an obvious shock for a child – especially from birth till the 4th year. A mother uses natural instincts and intuition to connect with her child. This does not apply in cases where the mother is depressed. If a mother misses this connection then the child will miss necessary care. 1) But if the father plays his role correctly and if the child receives care from its grandmother/s, the child will grow up with fear - a mild form of anxiety but not the paranoid anxiety that leads to depression. 2) If the father is alone with the depressed mother, without help from outside, the oldest of their girls will be martyrs and the youngest will have paranoid anxiety. In the case of boys, the oldest will be alcoholic and the youngest a cannabis abuser. 3) Say the mother is not depressed but is a career woman, and therefore lets the grandmother take care of her boy, subsequently gets a divorce and a new man, neglects her child through all of this; there is a 70 percent chance that the boy will become an addict. If the mother gets a divorce but doesn't remarry her daughters have borderline syndrome (pathological martyr). If she has boys, they will be lonely and melancholy. 4) If the mother is an alcoholic or drug addict, but the father can play his natural role, their self-centered boy will be a narcissist with an explosive temperament. So, this what happens when children grow up without necessary care from their parents. Let us now focus on how depression occurs in human beings.

A fundamental psychodynamic model by Freud espouses that when a child is missing his mother's care and when the mother cannot cope with the child's anxiety and transform this into something positive, the child will have a depression. An experiment that supports this theory is an attempt in the late 1990s - a young monkey is taken away from his mother. Under so much stress the little monkey produces an abundance of hormone and finally develops depression. However, this is an illogical example for the following reasons: In the animal world there is no father's role. Animals are polygamous, where one leader controls the group and has many females. The female protects her young while the male is often jealous and eats his young if he can get away with it (monkeys, lions, rabbits, etc.).

In human beings, fathers struggle for almost a year to establish real contact with their child through play, as they become aware that it is their duty to protect their child. This does not exist in the animal world, where the female tends to her young for about two years, after which it is left to fend for itself. But in human world the father, is of course, jealous of his newborn child, but (thankfully) does not kill and eat it. The father's feelings for the child gradually change and develop through play and protection. This is what animals are missing. To survive animals do not need a father but a mother who can teach them to fight for themselves.

According to the Sisifos method fathers play the central role in giving rise to depression, as demonstrated in late modern society, because men have lost their traditional dynamic role to women. In late modern society depression has now become the most common symptom. Where earlier the rate of depression was 2-3 percent, it is now almost 25 percent (for example, 30 percent of all women in France are on antidepressants). If the reader has doubts, we will discuss all this in great detail later while describing the therapeutic model.

Like I mentioned earlier, when a child misses care and love from the mother it is obviously traumatic. The child will not immediately develop depression, but a related symptom - melancholy. An anxious and stressed mother who complains and feels unfairly treated by society, ignored by her husband, creates a negative symbiosis for both mother and child - they cannot communicate and have no real contact with one another. This combination leads to a melancholic child. When the child, in this case a boy, grows up he will be lonely. He can have an education and get a good job but he cannot find a place in society and does not know what real friendship means. He is therefore unable to build a family. He is an adult physically but psychologically, he is a small, sweet boy who is grappling to deal with his traumatic past. This makes his mental age 9-10 years. If he gets married and has children, he will generally be very nice and sweet, but he will have temperamental outbursts full of aggression and anger, for even within his family he is lonely. If his wife has a good job, he will live with the phobia that she will leave him one day.

As a child, instead of going to his father (God) for help he tries to take responsibility for his parents' war and believes he can solve their issues through his own good behavior. For example, he will excel at school, help other students and have hobbies that he indulges in alone. In contrast, if he has depression at this age he will feel guilty and punish himself. In the melancholic boy's case, as an adult he will feel asexual, almost impotent. There is one exception to this – if the mother plays the masculine role, earns plenty of money and pressurizes the child too much to excel then he will grow up to be extremely sexual. If the mother is not dominant, stays home and spends a lot of time with the child, making him help out in the kitchen etc. then the boy will grow up to be a homosexual.

At school the child will always be a moppet, because he unable to express his opinion or speak his mind (to the dominant father - albeit in a child's eyes still represents God). When the child cannot express his opinions to the father he stays uncertain and confused and this has an important effect at school. Just as the child starts to maintain a distance from the father at home, he will unconsciously maintain a distance to the other children at school and start being a loner. This distance will unconsciously provoke the other children to bully and tease the child. When he feels unfairly treated and cries he feels, very unfortunately, that this treatment is just because he is a bad child and is guilty. The others treat him unfairly because he does not play with them. For the first time the child feels, according to him, punished fairly. So the guilt the child feels at home has now extended to the community and school.

The period during which the child expects this just punishment from the other children (bullying and teasing) is indescribably hard for the child. He cannot sleep at night and is constantly disappointed, lonely and crying, because he is not accepted by the other children. The only thing the child is waiting for is that his parents will one day save him. Usually this culminates in the parents switching schools for the child. But this will unfortunately serve to merely trigger the third fundamental characteristic of depression – the feeling of being a loser. The boy has not learned to fight in the old school and then the parents changed schools, so for the rest of his life this boy will expect another person to save his life and consequently never again express his opinion. It will start with the child remaining passive and expecting that a companion will take the initiative to say hello or to play. He will start to stress and become tense. He will accept that he is totally alone and has no desire to even eat with his parents at home. If eating with parents is a necessity then he will say that he does not like food. He will constantly try to do everything his parents want him too, but unfortunately they are occupied with everything else but their child.

As mentioned, the child's loneliness extends beyond school to home and slowly to all situations until the age of 15-16 years and then he is depressed. His demonstration is now taking a different form – it is a rebellion against society and its rules. The child does not come to school because he cannot wake up in the morning and does not want to shower -this episode lasts 2-3 months. Since these children are passive, they eat very little in some periods and lose a lot of weight, while in others they eat a lot and put on a lot of weight. After this first episode of 2-3 months turning the boy will turn back to his old life, until a new episode occurs when he is around 25 years old. If he is lucky it will occur when he is 30 years. This is the limit and this time it will be a period of real depression - the black zone.

Depression at the age of 14-16 years is expressed physically as well as mentally. Physically, through severe headaches, muscle aches, a sore solar plexus and abdomen. The psyche is reflected through hypochondria – the depressed push themselves a lot all the time, they can often have a heart attack (and usually survive it), inexplicable feeling of guilt and subjection to abstinence (from society and sex). When analyzed, all depressed people portray 7 characteristics: 1) They sleep in fits and wake up early, 2) lack of or excessive appetite, 3) reduced sexual desire, 4) lack of concentration and ability to remember the past, 5) low vocal pitch and monotonous tone, 6) pneumonia-like pain throughout the body, and 7) feelings of guilt and self-inflicted torture (suicide).

To sum up - depression occurs at the age of 7. The child feels guilty and punishes himself for it. He feels like a loser and an unavoidable depression is underway as early as the 8th year of a child's life. All symptoms have taken shape by the age of 14- 16 years when the boy experiences conflicts between objective reality and personal imagination. Depression is the only symptom that takes form very early in life – the child goes directly from the cause to the symptom, in other words there is no effect period. This type of depression is what we call classical or major depressive disorder (up until 1970). In late modern society, after the 1970s, depression has taken on a different form. The framework of society now needs people to be winners, not losers – there is no place for losers in society. This can be observed in a new symptom, which I call the double phase - endogenous-melancholy. I will expand on this later in the book.

I hope the preceding notes have given the reader an idea of what depression is. It is obviously a very important theme that I describe in greater detail in another book. The few things I have described here are fundamental in understanding how clients' psychology changes during the five stages of the therapeutic process.

When a child aged 14-16 years is involved in conflicts, the child begins to move from his own fantasy world and wishful thinking to the objective reality. The conflicts are usually with society and parents. From this point onwards two things could happen. The first is that child uses personal shortcomings and failures to build his own pragmatic ego – his ego is no longer dependent on his parents. The second is that the child develops what I described earlier as a 'Plasma' ego – the boy is unable to express his opinions and cannot stand up for himself.

Up until the 15th year every boy has his own problematic ego (dependent on the parents) and his psychosynthesis will be very different from other boys the same age - each boy has his own. When a child has a symptom though, it will remain forever and there will be no development. This is unlike a normal pragmatic ego which is continuously developing.

Development cycle of a pragmatic ego:

Phase	**Analysis**	**Synthesis**
Cause phase (0-9 years)	Nurturing and love from the mother Play-time and establishment of limits from the father	Dependent ego (from the parents) and untainted, positive outlook on life
Effect phase (9-12 years)	Unconditional love and support from the parents make the child fearless and create a curiosity for life	The child is very social and outgoing
Problematic ego (14-16 years)	At this point all children have a problematic ego. They now start to seek approval from their parents by imitating their behavior and then impress them by outdoing them – this is normal behavior. There is internal conflict and this conflict leads them to commit necessary mistakes which turn into personal development. A normal, pragmatic ego now develops.	

Development cycle of a symptom:

Phase	**Analysis**	**Synthesis**
Cause phase (0-9 years)	Lack of nurturing and love from the mother. And/or, Lack of play-time and establishment of limits from the father	Develops fears in the child – it will be afraid of the entire world
Effect phase (9-12 years)	The child is full of angst and is unsure of himself	The child is unsocial and begins to idolize the parents – it begins to either project fantasy stories to cover up or hides them from the world altogether. At this point the child will have one basic behavior characteristic.
Plasma ego (14-16 years)	The child begins to believe fantasies are reality and does not know the difference. The child cannot socialize or develop normally because its life is built on fantasy that other people believe to be the truth and in time so does the child. The line between fantasy and reality blurs. Therefore, there will be no personal development because the child is unable to move beyond this point into reality. A plasma ego has developed with seven distinct behavior characteristics.	

THE THERAPEUTIC APPROACH TO DEPRESSION

The treatment of depression is a part of the eternal struggle between psychiatry and psychology. Psychiatry supports the idea that it is possible to get an episode of depression without psychological stress. The pain and depression in general psychiatry may well be treated medically. This is in contrast to psychology and psychoanalysis, which sees depression as something that occurs as a result of trauma in childhood or as stemming from other underlying causes. Both psychiatry and psychology, however, agree on one thing - that the central nervous system in the brain produces two different hormones in depression, serotonin and norepinephrine, a mechanism related to the production of hormones that biology has not yet been able to explain. Psychology accepts that people under stress, such as the loss of a loved one or chronic alcohol or marijuana abuse, produce two hormones - serotonin and norepinephrine. This is hypothesis though, since production of these two hormones could also occur in other situations. But psychiatry supports this hypothesis, since it expects antidepressants to treat depression. However, nobody so far is known to have become completely healthy and free from depression through psychiatric treatment. The only success psychiatry has with medical treatment is to remove suicidal thoughts 70% of the time – but not the suffering that still exists deep inside the client and surfaces in different forms.. So, even while on medication, these people live a terrible life of waiting for the next period of suffering. The focus of psychiatrics or psychologists is to remove suicidal feelings through medication and they refer to this as therapy – I repeat that this does not remove the inner suffering.

Therefore the question arises how therapy is managed these days? It is a synthesis of both psychiatry and psychology; we first prescribe medicines to liberate people from their pain and then deal with their depression through dialogue therapy. Dialogue therapy does not work when clients feel pain. The problem is that it only works in theory not in practice, as depressed people suffer in their fantasy world built on guilt and misconceptions about fair punishment, and are unable to communicate through dialogue with their therapist for more than ten minutes at a time. They have not learnt how to draw conclusions early in their lives. In their minds they are blocked, for example, children aged 4-5 years repeatedly ask for something every day that they know they can't have, like candy. They have a manic, negative idea of what communicating with the world means. But when they hear a no or their therapist sets limits for them, they suffer and cry, but still feel treated fairly because they see themselves as evil people who should be punished fairly. Therefore they refuse to go to a psychologist or therapist who would simply want to punish them. But when they do not get help, they suffer from depression and feel even guiltier because they have not been to a psychologist or therapist. Therefore, the therapist's goal in the first phase is not dialogue, but to remove the client's bodily pain and suffering.

From what I've written so far, it is clear that the way therapy is currently conducted for depression is not successful. Depressed people suffer great pain, have negative thoughts about everything and live in a fantasy world filled with guilt and self-inflicted torture. Therefore they cannot listen, build guilt ridden fantasy stories and have suicidal thoughts, despite being treated fairly by society. This is a specific form of self-inflicted torture. The Sisifos method is based on dialogue therapy, where the starting point is the client's life here and now, ending with the client's childhood. Fundamentally, it is a psychoanalytic method. The therapist is part of the therapy and goes through a psychosynthesis together with the client, and the common meeting point between the therapist and client is Plato's truth point. When two opposing realities (client and therapist) meet then real communication takes place.

In order to conduct effective therapy a strategy is required. We divide this strategy into three different phases and different steps or tactics are employed in each phase. In total the three phases are divided into seven steps.

The first two steps use the Socratic 'Mother Earth' method (to generate or conceive the client's internal truth, except during a depression). In the third and fourth steps, we use Plato's division method, in the fifth sixth and seventh steps a combination of shared methods and at the end the Aristotle method. We use the Sisifos method to deal with all the different symptoms, but the technique differs from symptom to symptom. The technique with which we treat the symptom, while logically selected by us in terms of our role as a therapist, is the result of how a client perceives and communicates with the world. For example an alcoholic thinks that society is unjust, so he is constantly complaining about the injustice of the world, and our job as therapists can be compared to an alcoholic as we prepare ourselves to go into battle. For example, when an alcoholic comes into my clinic for therapy I extend a hand although I know that alcoholics are against physical contact. I will not let the hand drop down, but with the same hand kindly show the client to where he will sit, while putting my left hand gently on his shoulder (as a loving father or mother would). This is not just a detail, but a fundamental technique in the therapeutic process for alcoholism. It is about showing them who the boss is. If I do not use this technique the alcoholic will become too familiar and provoke me, almost as if he is ready to fight. Only one other type of client comes into therapy with the same roaring, self-confident behavior as an alcoholic and that is a narcissist (a very self-confident, self-centered person who thinks he always right and is a born winner). Narcissists do not familiarize and provoke as alcoholics, but are typically the center of the room and always seek attention. In other words, with narcissists we have no need to go into battle, but can only ask them to take a seat and begin dialogue. I choose to mention these two specific but different symptoms, as they have some common characteristics. A therapist can also find it difficult to distinguish one from the other unlike marijuana addiction which is a completely different type of psychosynthesis. A marijuana addict is not there to win or to fight because they are typically defeatists.

The most important rule of therapy is therefore, in contrast to much of the rest of psychology, to diagnose a symptom in the first meeting itself. The therapy is used as a tool to diagnose the symptom. Unfortunately, it is not always so easy to diagnose and classify different symptoms. This can be especially difficult when it comes to depression. There is more darkness woven in here than any other symptom.

There are two categories of basic symptoms that have depressive characteristics but are commonly misdiagnosed as depression.

Category 1 - being a martyr and melancholy. These two disorders have some common characteristics that lead people to generalize and not see the differences, and therefore classify them under a common heading as depression.

Category 2 – Heroin users, marijuana users, anxiety, anorexic/bulimic and narcissists. Compared to the first category there still greater confusion here, since these five symptoms are not in the depression 'family', but have depressive phases that can act as a façade and be misleading. So instead of diagnosing that a client suffers from marijuana addiction a confused therapist dealing with a marijuana addict's depressed phase believes that his overall symptom is depression. Let's see how this is reflected in practice.

In 2004, the municipality psychologists questioned why only ten percent of all marijuana addicts in Denmark completed their therapy. The psychologist unions replied that the psychologists were trying to conduct therapy for depression, because their clients had not said that they used marijuana. If you are confused as all psychologists and psychiatrists are it is very understandable, since depression is a phase in a marijuana user's symptom and not the overall symptom itself. The client's body language will clearly show that the client is suffering from a marijuana addiction and not classical depression. If the therapist is able to distinguish the different forms of depression and diagnosis, he can conduct therapy successfully but not otherwise.

In the following pages I provide ten real-life illustrations of how difficult it is to diagnose and differentiate when a person suffers from what we call classical major depression, or when it is symptoms that have an embedded depression phase.

The first three examples are Greek women from the post-Second World War period who underwent therapy with me:

1. A 35-year-old female high school teacher with two children, one and three years old respectively. She comes in asking for help because she has got divorced and subsequently has been very depressed. She is a well-dressed woman but crying constantly because she cannot understand why her divorced husband will not have the children every weekend. The woman's father was a communist and at the end of the war, participated in the civil war against the fascists and conservatives. Our client, Maria, was born in the fifties, after the civil war. Her father remained in prison for 10 years after her birth. Maria has only seen her father after she was 10 years old. After a harsh time in prison, her father was not physically able to work and was treated like a stigmatized communist. Therefore, Maria's mother had to work as a nurse at the local hospital and supported the entire family.

Maria met her ex-husband Petro five years ago, but did not tell Petro about her father's communist past. Petro owns a small export company and is apolitical. After a year Maria realizes that her husband is unable to maintain a family. She begins to learn this during her first pregnancy, when she does not get help from Petro, who also works in the evening. Maria is very disappointed and bitter with Petro, but despite this, she chooses to have another baby with him. As she says in therapy she had forgiven him and wanted to give him a second chance. But unfortunately Petro is even more distant through the second pregnancy and she is even more alone than she was during the first birth. After the second birth, she is very depressed and weeps constantly.

Instead of helping, Petro is aggressive and maintains his distance, and therefore Maria decides to divorce him after she is able to work again. Unfortunately, things do not improve for Maria after the divorce because she now believes that Petro is a hard man and has no feelings for her or the children. In the first period after the divorce Petro lives with his parents and has no room to invite their children over for weekends. It is very difficult for him to have the children sleep over so he brings the children back to Maria in the evenings. Maria feels that she is in a prison where she does not have a single day free. She divorced her husband when he did not show sympathy and compassion or contribute to the children's upbringing, but she hoped that things would get better after the divorce. In reality it is the opposite; the situation worsens because she now manages two children and a job alone – the only reason she goes on and does not commit suicide is for the sake of the children.

This example is typical of what many psychologists and psychiatrists call 'second postnatal depression'. But is this really true? Does Maria really suffer from depression or from other psychological symptoms?

2. A 30-year-old divorced mother, Elleni, has a five year old daughter. Elleni is a violin coach and has a boyfriend but they don't live together. She comes in to see me because 'things are very, very hard and I have depression.' She says her boyfriend never does anything to take care of her or her girl. He cannot decide whether they should live together and they have sex only twice a month. When I ask her in therapy why she will not leave him because they apparently have nothing in common (they do not live together, do not share interests and have no sex life) she replies that she is in love with him and therefore cannot be separated from him.

Elleni's father was a fascist and with the block that won the civil war. He was very violent - he beat her mother and Ellini since she was five years old. Elleni feels very depressed and talks in a low voice holding in her body like a small, wounded cat. When I ask about her relationship with her father she says that she knows that her father was a fascist psychopath, but she has never understood why her father was so aggressive when she disagreed with him.

For example, her father was not consenting of her marriage to her former husband. But she cannot understand why her father and husband quarreled when they invited her father to visit. She does not understand why her father was so aggressive when she separated from her husband. Now she is afraid to tell her father that she has a boyfriend who she does not live with. When her father hears this he will call her a whore. When Ellini speaks she has no emotion in her voice, just a constant, low monotone. She says that nobody understands her and feels very alone and depressed. She has no energy or desire to plan for the future.

Is Elleni's symptom depression or something else?

3. A 50-year-old divorced woman named Sofia has lived alone for the past 15 years. She has a daughter, Xenia, aged 20. Sofia is separated from her husband because he was paranoid and beat her. Sofia's father was a German soldier during the occupation of Greece and her mother became pregnant during their first and only night of love. At this time, Sofia's mother lived with her parents in a small town with 5000 inhabitants. Sofia grandparents could not accept that their daughter was pregnant by a German soldier and threw her on to the streets.

Sofia's mother then came to Athens. Here she tried for the first year to cope with life, alone with little Sofia, but this is very hard for her. Therefore, she invited her 18 year old sister to Athens and told her that she needs to take Sofia back with her and bring her up. So, Sofia grew up in a small town with her grandparents and her aunt pretending to be her mother. But everyone in the small town was aware that Sofia is not the aunt's child and Sofia is stigmatized. Sofia does not feel her aunt's husband is her father. He has no love for her and at the age of 12 years, she learns the truth that her aunt is not her mother.

One evening, when Sofia is 13, her real mother comes to the village and offers to take Sofia back with her to Athens, where she has found a man who accepts that Sofia is the daughter of a German soldier. Sofia refuses, despite the fact that she does not feel good being with her aunt - later in therapy she actually says that her uncle (playing father) loved his dog more than her. She could not accept her mother's act of abandoning her. At the age of 15 year Sofia leaves the small town after being mobbed at school for being the bastard child of a German soldier. She makes contact with her mother and chooses to stay with her. But she still finds it hard to forgive her mother and after three years leaves her.

She begins a relationship with a paranoid artist who is very aggressive. They marry and for first eight years do not live together all the time as the man travels a lot. Each time he comes back she is afraid that he will beat her. Finally the police come to the rescue and with their help she leaves him. The last five years have been very difficult for her. She cannot work or make enough retirement money to survive. She feels guilty because she cannot forgive her mother and she could not protect her own daughter against a violent father. So what are her symptoms? Is it depression?

I have had three other female clients, who all came from Norway, and whose fathers were German soldiers during World War II, who reacted exactly the same way as Sofia in the third example. This type of symptom is very prevalent in countries where there has been war or armed conflict.

4. A 50-year old divorced woman, Julia, has lived alone since she gave birth to her daughter. She asks for help because she can only work three to five months a year as a medical secretary and therefore feels guilty that for the rest of the year she must live from state unemployment funds.

5. 55-year old Katherine, a mother of three who lives with her husband. At the age of 30 years she could not work anymore because of depression. She has been hospitalized twice - the first time when she was 37 years for six months and again at 40 years for three months.

6. Anders is 30 years old and is a school teacher. Anders has depression and has not been able to work the last year.

7. Pernille is 20 years old and has dropped out of art academy after the first year because of depression.

8. Mikkel is 34 years old, an actor and a lot more. He has been able to cope with his job but not with relationships.

9. Torben, a 47-year-old unemployed artist from the music world who has been medicated for 10 years with antidepressants. When he comes in, he has been divorced for the third time. He has three children with three different women.

10. A very aggressive man, George, who feels constantly disappointed by people who do not understand him. He is tired of other people's stupidity. He is the father of two children and lives with his wife.

All the details that I have about clients, I obtain within the first two months of therapy.

THERAPY

1. Maria's therapy

During the first session, I learn that Maria comes to me with the hope of completely removing her husband from her life after the divorce, but at the same time accuses Petro of not spending enough time with the children.

Dialogue therapy

Therapist: Maria, can you explain to me why you worry so much that your children can not see their father every weekend. Is it for your own sake or out of concern for the children?
Maria (responds with tears in his eyes): Of course for the children's sake. When I'm alone with them they ask where their father is and I do not know what to tell them.
Therapist: O.k., when you do not know what to say, what do you do?
Maria: I tell them the truth that their father does not live with us anymore. He lives with his mother. But when my children ask why their father lives with his mother and not with us, I do not know what to say (Maria starts weeping).

We pause, Maria drinks a glass of water, and continue:
Therapist: So Maria, if I understand you correctly, your problem is not that you do not know what to say to the children, but that you are afraid to tell your children about being officially divorce. Am I right?
Maria (earnestly): Yes, that is my problem. I do not want to hurt my children.
Therapist: O.k. Maria, so what are you thinking you'll do - keep the divorce a secret from your children?
Maria: No, I want to tell them but without hurting them.
Therapist: O.k. Maria, bravo, for it is true that you say we must inform children about a divorce, so we agree on that. Let's find out how you can best inform your children. But you must not think that this can be done without any sorrow or pain for your children, because as you know, one

needs to break an egg to make an omelet. But Maria, I have a question for you - Why is it you who needs to inform the children and not your husband Petro?
Maria: It's probably because it is me who has taken the decision to divorce, so it is I who must inform the children.
Therapist: Yes, but did you get divorced to hurt your children or to feel better about yourself since your husband was not involved with you or their upbringing?
Maria: I chose to get divorced because I could not handle more. I was ready. But now I worry a lot about how I'll explain this to my children.
Therapist: This means that when you divorced your husband, you had not thought about how it would affect your children. Are you sure that you have really made the right choice to divorce your husband, because we cannot avoid hurting our children when we separate. Can you handle it?
Maria: No, I cannot handle it. Petro acts like a small child. No more. The end. I cannot accept him keeping a distance from the children. It is too hard for me.

This kind of dialogue therapy with Maria takes two months. In these two months Maria is accusatory and aggressive towards her husband, because she is afraid to tell the children about the divorce together with Petro. Maria has the same phobia now from when the children at school teased her about her father being in prison, even though she knew from her mother that her father was not a criminal, but a communist who fought for human rights. She did not know how she to defend her father in front of the other children. So now, Maria is afraid to inform the children together with Petro, because if Petro says, 'Your mother took the decision to divorce', she won't know what to say, for it is the truth. Maria unconsciously projects her guilt on to her husband. She weeps and accuses her husband because she herself does not know what she should say to her children. Maria exercised the right to divorce, but she did not prepare herself for the consequences of her decision in relation to the children. It shocks her because she experienced the same thing when her father was in prison and she was alone. She projects the same pain for her children. When she gets divorced she takes Petro away from the children's lives and therefore she feels guilty.

After two to three months of therapy she is able to liberate herself from guilt. Now Maria stops pressurizing herself. She begins to understand that Petro did not move in with his mother to hurt her (Maria), but because he had no money and therefore could not look after their children. Petro never wanted to be apart from Maria and it has been a shock for him. He even had to close down his export business. After the divorce Maria begins to understand that she should not give orders to her man, as if they were together, but that she must speak with respect to him, so she does not destroy the children's image of their father as a God.

After 7 months of therapy Maria understands that it was her own choice to marry Petro and have children and that she should not have looked upon him as if he was just a little boy. After Maria's father's release from prison she has had the constant phobia that one day she will again lose her father to a police arrest. Maria is confused by two realities: one from her father that communism is the only right and capitalism is wrong - and the other reality: communism is wrong and capitalism is right. She was teased at school because she was the only one with a communist background.

Maria experienced a major trauma early in her life - to live without a father. After her father's release this trauma did not disappear, but worsened because she was teased at school. Maria unconsciously always wanted to start a family with someone like Petro who did not have a communist background. She takes a decision to move past her father's communist past and believes that if she chooses an apolitical husband her children will not experience the same harsh treatment as she did. Being with Petro was not wrong but unfortunately she chose the wrong reasons to be with him.

After 9 months of therapy Maria is not only fighting back but also learning to pay the price – in other words face consequences. For example, when she married Petro she would take decisions alone, not together with him. So when Petro's business started to go badly, instead of supporting him so together they could cope with the slump, she decided to leave him. Maria abandons things by applying an either-or logic:
1. Petro is not a good father and does not participate in their children's upbringing.
2. Petro's business has gone bad.
Conclusion: Maria need to divorce Petro

She would have acted correctly if she had:
1. Invited Petro into the lives of the children in the form of duties
2. Supported her husband, 'If your company is not doing well you'll find something else'
3. Supported him the same way she has supported her father. Maria should not have separated from Petro, but helped him by sharing the slump with him and making him a part of the family.

Maria finished her therapy when she saw her father's negative sides and accepted them. When she was ready to say, 'Father, why are you not able to understand that I did not like it when you didn't teach me to defend myself when all the children in class teased me. Where were you when I was alone and was bullied?' Maria grew up with guilt and felt like a traitor when she was 14 and couldn't defend the fact that what her father said was the opposite of what society said to the other children. Maria will be free from fear and confusion when she puts her father and her ego in the right place. The civil war has ended and we should not continue as if it was her parents' war. Maria was a communist because of her father - it was never her choice. But she learned to keep it a secret as an adult - and therefore she chose to be with Petro.

Elleni's therapy

Elleni comes in so that I can help her take a decision whether she should get divorced or not. In the first two months I try to open up Elleni's inner world or reality. Elleni plays a role; she is not in therapy to get better. She comes in show how much she suffers and what a good a heart she has to be able to forgive all of her ex-boyfriends' bad behavior and actions. The first two months of therapy take shape as follows:

Elleni: I do not understand why, when my husband comes home he does not play with our daughter but sits alone and plays the guitar.
Therapist: But have you asked him about it? Have you asked Kostas why he sits around and plays the guitar?
Elleni: Noooo (in a cat-like purr), because I expect that he should understand it himself.
Therapist: So how much time do you think he needs to understand this –that he needs to play with his daughter rather than play his guitar?
Elleni: Nooo (again in a cat-like purr), this will hurt my daughter.
(Her answer made no sense and was out of context)
Therapist: Wow (acting surprised)! You are a fantastic mother, congratulations! I've never experienced a mother who could love her daughter as much as you.
Elleni: Hmm. Yes (arrogantly), I love my daughter so much. The worst thing I can imagine is hurting my daughter.
Therapist: Well done, congratulations! But have you made Kostas aware about this great love you have for your daughter?
Elleni: Yes, but not in as many words as you say it.
Therapist: So, what do you do while Kostas plays music and your daughter is alone? This must be a huge dilemma for you?
Elleni: I am there of course with my daughter, but you know what happens then? Kostas gets offended! Therefore I cannot do more and we must part.
Therapist: That's right. You suffer a lot. But that's why you're here - to learn how to tackle dilemmas without getting a divorce.

This dialogue takes place in the first two months. Elleni lives in a fantasy world and cannot distinguish fantasy from reality. She is unable to feel the inner core logic, and as a mother first and foremost protect her daughter, Maria. She must choose a husband who can support her daughter, not a man like Kostas, who competes with her daughter. This happens because she has never seen her father as a positive person. Her father beat her when she was 5 years and older and she has never been able to communicate well with him. She has not had any support from her mother, but instead experienced maternal guilt being thrown towards her. So Elleni experienced terror every single day, very early in her life. She is afraid to express her feelings for her father because he beat her.

After two months of therapy Elleni learns that she should not speak like an artificial machine to her daughter, for example, 'Come here sweetheart, now we must eat.' She must show in practice how life really is, 'Today I am a little tired after work and have no energy, so lets have a quiet meal together.' Another day she may say, 'Hooray! Today I am very happy. We will sing while we eat'.

After five months of therapy Elleni began to understand that she must take the initiative to show Kostas that he cannot play offense against her daughter, but participate in the Maria's upbringing. He cannot stop her if she wants to play, dance, etc. She also stop needs him to stop smoking marijuana because he has no energy or good sense thereafter.

After nine months of therapy Elleni confesses that she was the victim of rape at 16 and 18 years. Elleni also confesses that she was unfaithful to her first husband and divorced him, not because he was a drug addict (as she earlier claimed) but because she chose to be with another man.

After 12 months of therapy has Elleni learned to make room for her boyfriend and play her role as a woman. If Kostas does not want sex, she must tell him that their relationship does not work, and that they must move on from each other instead of finding a new boyfriend and being unfaithful, as she has been so many times before.

After 15 months of therapy, Elleni confronts her parents with her malice. She then starts maintaining a distance from them and begins a new life. Not in her imagination but in reality. Kostas stops smoking marijuana and they move on together to build a new life as a real family.

Sofia's therapy

Sofia speaks with no emotion in her voice and weeps constantly. The left side of her body is sore and she has no energy or desires. She wants to commit suicide.

The first two months of therapy dialogue

Sofia: I am alone in the world. I do not know when it is morning and when it is evening. I stay home and do not like to go out to shop. I cannot stand people.
Therapist: That's true – I can see that you have no energy. How long have you been in this situation? 40 days…60 days…6 months…?
Sofia: I don't remember. Because it feels it has been like this my whole life.
Therapist: Can you remember if you have had a fever at any time in the recent past?
Sofia: No, I do not remember.
Therapist: Can you remember what you ate the day before yesterday or three days ago?
Sofia: No, I do not remember.
Therapist: O.k., I understand your situation. Just one last question: Who have you talked with lately?
Sofia: With my daughter. But I cried when we talked.
Therapist: O.k., I don't want to hear about your discussion, because I know it is hard for you. But when did you last see your mother, Sofia?
Sofia: I do not remember, maybe one or two years ago. But I do not like to call her, because she feels guilty and cries constantly. She apologizes to me all the time and is paranoid. She speaks in a delirium about her

mother and father who died many years ago. My father died five years ago and my mother is alone, 85 years old and paranoid.
Therapist: Have you forgiven your mother, Sofia, because she slept with a German soldier?
Sofia: I think I have, but I have no feelings for her. Maybe I have not.
Therapist: Do you feel guilty about your daughter, because you did not protect her when your husband beat her?
Sofia: Yes, I cannot sleep at night. I often wake up every two hours and it has been that way for almost ten years now.
Therapist: Are you taking an antidepressant?
Sofia: The last ten years, Yes. I started with 10mg, went to 20mg and now I take 50 mg of Efecsor® or Seroxat®.

The first two months I work to free my clients from guilt. Sofia feels guilty because she has been lonely since she was five years old. She could not understand why her uncle gave his dog more attention than her. She could not understand why her mother left her and came back to take her when she was 13 years old.

We can use the example of the judgment of King Solomon from the Old Testament to help Sofia understand her mother:
Two new mothers approach Solomon, bringing with them one dead and one live baby boy. Each mother presents the same story and accusation: She and the other woman live together and have both recently given birth to baby boys. One night, soon after the birth of their respective boys, one woman woke to find that she had smothered her own baby in her sleep. In anguish and jealousy, she took her dead son and exchanged it with the other's child. The following morning, the woman discovered the dead baby and soon realized that it was not her own son, but the other woman's.

After some deliberation, King Solomon calls for a sword to be brought before him. He declares that there is only one fair solution: the live son must be split in two, each woman receiving half of the child. Upon hearing this terrible verdict, the boy's true mother cries out, "Please, My Lord, give her the live child—do not kill him!" However, the liar, in her bitter jealousy exclaims, "It shall be neither mine nor yours—divide it!" Solomon instantly gives the live baby to the real mother, realizing that the true mother's instincts were to protect her child, while the liar revealed that she did not truly love the child.

Dialogue therapy continues:
Therapist: Sofia, your mother did the right thing: She gave you to her sister in order to survive. Your mother was stigmatized because nobody would accept that she was pregnant with a German soldier during the occupation.

Dialogue Therapy from 2nd to 4th month:
Therapist: When you speak with your mother on the phone and understand that she is paranoid and in her own world, how do you feel?
Sofia: Very bad.
Therapist: Why do you feel very bad? I do not understand you.
Sofia: But umm (she stammers) what shall I do, should I be happy?
Therapist: No, but your mother is old and she feels guilty because she left you. And in one way or another, we can see things aren't so good for her because she is lonely. For example, the only contact she has with you is three times per year on the phone. Her world is very small. Do you agree?
Sofia: Yes, yes, I agree, she does not get to see many people. And I keep her at a distance as well.
Therapist: So maybe that is why you feel bad - because you do not have real contact with your mother?
Sofia: But what shall I say to her? She is paranoid.
Therapist: It's not about what you'll say Sofia, but about the emotions you show her.
Sofia: But are you sure that it will help my mother get better if I show emotions?
Therapist: You have a point Sofia, if you show emotions she might not get better, but I am 100 percent confident that you will feel better and

never feel guilty.
Sofia: Hmmm, I see. I never thought of it that way before.
Therapist: Yes, Sofia. For example, you told me before that you have forgiven your mother, but have you ever told her that you love her?
Sofia: No, no, never. I cannot say that to her, because I do not love her - she ruined my life.
Therapist: Sofia, sorry, but if you that's the way you think then you have not really forgiven your mother. It is just words but not reality or in practice.
Sofia (breaks down and starts weeping): How can I forgive her, when 500,000 Greeks lost their lives during the German occupation and she finds one of these monsters and makes him my father, a Nazi father.

We pause, I give Sofia a glass of water and continue:

Therapist: O.k. Sofia, breathe deep. Breathe in from your mouth and down into your stomach and when you're ready, we will continue. Sofia, I agree with you completely. What your mother did was unacceptable. My own father, Sofia, fought against the Germans and Italians during the occupation, and I personally fought against the military government in Greece from 1977-78. You have the right to be aggressive and it is very, very hard to forgive her. But Sofia, it is not our objective to make your mother pay for the consequences for her mistake. Why do put yourself at the same level as your mother and why are you in such a small world, just as your mother? You are alone, you have no contact with your daughter, no friends and you are depressed.
Sofia: I do not know.
Therapist: Maybe because you feel guilty, first, because as a 13-year-old girl you refused to go back to your mother when she came to fetch you from your aunt. And second, because you lived with her till you were 18 but only to set her up for 3 years of failure so you could leave her abruptly. And lastly, because your father was not a stupid Nazi but maybe a passive and weak man. We do not know because you have never met him, Sofia, and you have never learned who your father is

In that moment I realize that it is necessary for Sofia to find out who her father is. She also understands that it is crucial - she must seek out various German organizations, etc. to learn the truth about her father. In this way I can put the automatic Nazi label in doubt and at the same time give her some hope.
Therapist: So, because you felt guilty and wanted to punish yourself you chose a paranoid and sadistic man. And you did not divorce him despite the fact that he was that way for so many years. Your depression is a combination of your guilt and self-inflicted torture.

When Sofia's husband hit her and her daughter, Sofia believed that they deserved it because she was a pitiable person with only herself to blame and therefore saw no need to leave him. The first time Sofia thought of divorce was after 10 years of being with her husband – one day she saw her daughter's face completely bloody after a beating from her husband. We continued this dialogue from the 2nd to 4th month of therapy, so Sofia learnt to distinguish between the guilt stemming from her mother's actions and her own.

1. Sofia's mother had the right to feel guilty and is now paying the consequences for her mistake (having a child with a German soldier).
2. Sofia did nothing wrong by rebelling against her mother twice, first as a 13 and then a 15 year old. So why should she feel guilty?
3. In the period since then Sofia acted like a little wounded child who is suffering a lot. Why is she, now a 50-year-old woman, not free from her guilt? She is no longer a child but a 50-year-old woman.

Sofia feels free from guilt and grief for the first time in her life after she tells her mother she loves her, understands what really happened and truly forgives. A very emotional liberation takes place between mother and daughter, and for the first time in their lives they talk to each other as mother and daughter. So Sofia is for the first time free from her guilt towards her mother. She feels strong and like a winner, and begins to recognize her own feelings, which give her energy and dynamism. She begins to think and make plans, inter alia, to build a future. For example, she spends Christmas with her mother - they cook, have fun and laugh together, rather than cry and feel sorrow as before. But Sofia still feels guilty about her daughter because she couldn't protect her from a violent father:

1. Why did she choose to be with such a monster?
2. Why did she not divorce him when he beat her daughter in front of her?

Therapy for this is less complicated and lasts 5 to 6 months. This time it's easier to free her from guilt. I analyze Sofia as a woman who is the victim of a violent man, who paralyzes her and because she is in a depression, she keeps it a secret and feels ashamed. Many women without any symptoms do not report their violent men to the police. So if she should feel guilty about something it should be because she was too weak to call the police, and not because she has ruined her daughter as she unfortunately imagines. The only one who has real reason for guilt is her psychopathic ex-husband because he beat Sofia and her daughter.

To relieve a person from guilt we need to show them the source of the guilt and how it came about. After 7 months Sofia is free of all guilt and for the first time in her life she must fight to create a different but healthy relationship with her daughter. Up until now we have analyzed Sofia, but what about her daughter, Maria? Which of the two parents did she choose to be with and why? What is her symptom? If you think that Maria chose to stay with her mother because she was the victim of her father, you are wrong. Maria chooses distance and hates her mother because she has been unable to protect Maria from her father. Maria is also a woman, and therefore subject to the Oedipus complex, and this is why she admires her father.

At the age of 15 Maria goes to Rome to live with her father. She discovers that her father is a kind of gigolo and this is very hard on her.

She cannot understand her love for her father and so many arguments begin. Maria has many pictures of her father but cannot assemble them into a whole. She begins to feel disgusted by her father, while she loves him. She hates her mother. She begins to eat a lot and throw it up - her symptom develops - bulimia. To help Sofia it is also necessary to help her family. Therefore Maria also begins therapy with. Not common therapy with mother and daughter, but two separate, private therapies. After nine months of therapy with Sofia, she is able to set limits on her daughter Maria. Whenever Sofia went on a date with a new man, she was always afraid of Maria's struggle and jealousy towards the new man. And Sofia does not allow her ex-husband to visit her and Maria at home. Only in the event that he apologizes for his violent actions against the two women (which no psychopath has until now) will he be allowed to visit.

After 14 months of therapy Sofia is like a re-born girl of 15-16, who begins to dream of a prince on a white horse who will come to her. She begins to be happy and sees life positively. Therapy is complete after 18 months when Sofia understands that she is 50 years old, and the prince is an old one without a horse. But she is now ready to accept a rhythm of life that suits her age.

4. Julia's therapy

Julia met her husband when she was 20 and they went on to live together for a year. After getting pregnant she left her husband. After their daughter was born she never managed to build a relationship with another man. She usually has one night stands or relationships that last a week or at most a month. She has been hospitalized three times, at the age of 30, 35 and finally at 39. Julia has taken antidepressants since she was 30 up until now (50). She has tremendous amounts of anxiety, numerous phobias and suffers from hypochondria. The first thing she says in dialogue therapy is that she has a terrible stomach ache and has suffered from this for 30 years even though she takes medication for it. She asks if I can liberate her from or heal this terrible pain. Instead of answering, I ask:

Therapist: The tests that you have undergone Julia, show that your pain is not physical, but psychological, and the cause is anxiety and stress. Is this true?
Julia: What do you mean - stress? Yes, stress is what I have; stress is what has made my life equivalent to death for so many years.
Therapist: O.k., our starting point is good because we are aware that your problem is completely psychological i.e. no pathological, natural causes (gastritis etc.).
Julia: How is that a good start? Poor me - this pain drives me crazy and I don't know what to do.
Therapist: Well, I call it a good start because at least you are not suffering from lung cancer or a fatal disease, because in those situations, I cannot help. So let's see, when it hurts, how does it come about and how long does it last?
Julia: I do not know. Since I was quite small, I have suffered and I can't anymore.

She starts crying, we pause and I give Julia a little water to drink. Then I continue:

Therapist: I request you to stop mentioning your childhood for a while and instead focus on life today. Can you tell me how it feels when you have pain? Can you breathe? And afterwards, when you breathe in again, does it feel like you have fire in your stomach?
Julia: Yes, exactly, that's the way I've felt since I was a toddler.
Therapist (I respond like a small child): Ah ah, I see, but remember what I said - not from your past when you were a child, but only about today.
Julia: Yes, uh, yes it is true for now as well, just now.
Therapist: O.k., besides a stomach ache do you have any sense of feeling in your fingers?
Julia: No, I haven't had that since I was a child.
Therapist: Hmm, again the same thing Madam, you reply from your past - from when you were a child. Therefore, allow me to explain why you should not answer with reference to your past, for example: which pain

came first, the stomach or the numbness in your fingers? Can you remember?
Julia: No, I just have pain in my body.

She starts crying again. We take a short break. This time I don't give water, but show her a breathing exercise. She needs to use it when she suffers a lot. After five minutes when she is a bit better, I continue.

Therapist: Third and final question, Madam Julia - Do you also suffer from headaches and strong migraines?
Julia: Yes, yes, I have suffered throughout my body and had migraines since I was a toddler.

This was the kind of dialogue at the first meeting; Julia discovers that there are three different kinds of pain in her body and not just one. She panics and cries all the time. In the first two months my aim is that Julia must learn how to deal with her various kinds of pain. Julia must learn to block out the negative which makes her panic and cry, and look at the positive side of life. I explain to Julia, for example, that we as human beings, beyond the physical, somatic immune system also have a psychological immune system. So when she has a stomach ache, she needs to breathe in through her mouth and down into the stomach. In this way, her stomach problems will go away after a while. Secondly, since she has not had a heart attack but has suffered so much pain, stress and anxiety since she was a child, it means that her body is physically and psychologically capable of handling anxiety and stress. These two points - the stomach ache and labored breathing, was my goal in the first months of therapy. Julia needed to be free from these two pains. I am aware that Julia is a hypochondriac and that she thinks she has stomach or lung cancer and is afraid of having heart attack. Once she is free from these physical pains, Julia will be able to express psychological pain without crying and getting desperate. When she feels pain again she does not panic or get anxious, but begins to respond positively to the pain. After three months Julia is able to have good discussions about her everyday life and problems without digressing. She has had anxiety and suffers a lot in her job because she constantly surrounded by ill people (she is a medical secretary). She cannot sleep at night because she constantly reminded of these people.

Therapist: Julia, I am very impressed because you offer sympathy and empathy to sick people. When we are sick and visit the doctor, we get even sicker when we see all the other sick people. It is a normal psychological response. But there is something missing here. And we will try to find that today.
Julia: I do not understand what you mean, Panos?
Therapist (in an explanatory tone): O.k., you have this half picture in your mind Julia - sick people suffer. You forgot to finish this picture though. For example, what happens to all those sick people when they have been to the doctor? Do they die or do they get better?
Julia: I don't know because I don't see them the next day.
Therapist: So, you never see them again?
Julia: Yes, yes, I see them again after a while, maybe one or two years.
Therapist: So, that means they are not dead but alive. It also means that the people you weep for in the evenings are not dead but alive.
Julia: Yes, yes, but do you think it is very satisfying to constantly see small children crying with a stomach ache?
Therapist: No, certainly not Madam, you're right - it is hard. But I'm asking you if they are better when they come back after a while?
Julia: Again, I do not understand what you mean.
Therapist: Julia, what is best for little sick children, as you suggesr to stay home and suffer and cry about their problems or to go the doctor and get some treatment? What is best?
Julia: Well, it is obviously preferable that they visit the doctor.
Therapist: Then that is what you must place in front of you today Julia, to complete the picture. That people who are sick visit the doctor for treatment. So, you can tell yourself to sleep well for this is a logical conclusion. Madam Julia, I have another question for you - you suffer and have so much fear of your job, then how do you manage to work continuously all year?

Julia: No, no, I work only five or six months a year, and at most three months in a row. I cannot handle more, it is too much.

She begins crying again, we take a break and she drinks some water. Then I continue:

Therapist: That's good Julia, that you take breaks from your job. Can you remember what we talked about earlier, that people have a psychological immune system? Your psychological immune system works well! I am very glad that you take these breaks.
Julia: Why do you say that? I should be happy? I feel terribly guilty because other people usually work 11 months a year.
Therapist: Why do you feel guilty if you choose to break for a holiday or because you cannot handle your job for extended periods? For example, if you were not psychologically so tired and suffering in your job, would you think of quitting or continuing to work all year round as other people do?
Julia: If I had the right psychological mindset I would never take breaks and live off social security.

I continue the dialogue but it should be noted that the client has understood where her guilt comes from:
1. Julia works three or five months a year, but suffers a lot on the job.
2. When she cannot cope with more psychological stress she is supported by state welfare.
Conclusion: She has not done anything wrong or illegal so needn't feel guilty. Her problem is that she cannot handle her job.
In the 5th to 7th month of therapy it is my goal to liberate Julia from her guilt towards her daughter and other family members. From the 7th to 9th month I free Julia from her guilt towards her parents. Julia is able to transfer her guilt to her parents and is free from depression. Julia will never be totally deprived of guilt, but after 15 months of therapy she has learnt how to defend herself against guilt. She suffers and cries no longer and is free from her symptoms. She will have a better relationship with

her daughter and grandson, but is still unable to start a new relationship with a man and share her life with him. Unlike earlier when the guilt was unbearable, now she accepts guilt and is able to feel good.

If Julia's therapy seemed harsh, the following example of Katherine is much worse. This therapy can be likened to a blow to the stomach. There were many times when I reached my own limits and was ready to give up. Therapists are sometimes victims of their own self-confidence and believe that they are something special. In this regard I am very grateful for therapy with Katherine because she brought me down to earth. I could not understand her actions and reactions, even though I already had considerable experience from many of my other depressed clients.

5. Katherine's therapy

Katherine is now 58 years old now and has been depressed since she was 30. When Katherine was first admitted to hospital for depression, her children were aged 14, 12 and 10 years. The 14 year old girl, now an adult, is a high school teacher. The second child, a boy, is an alcoholic, does nothing and has no education. Her third son is a lumberjack and smokes marijuana every weekend. All three children have seen a psychologist in their teens. When Katherine was in the hospital, her husband would watch all three children alone. Katherine was a special case because she, besides the guilt she got from her parents as a child, also had a great sense of guilt for being a mother who traumatized her children by making them see their mother being hospitalized.

Instead of love and care she gave her children negative emotions and created a thousand questions about why she had to be hospitalized. She had no answer for all these issues and so felt like an outsider in the family. Therefore, she wears no expression on her face, has no emotion in her voice and lives in another world filled with ghosts and guilt. She is unable to talk to anyone in the family and has also started to rave. For example, on her way to the toilet in hospital she mumbles senseless questions to others patients about an inconsequential television program. She mutters these questions to herself, opens the door to the toilet and goes in without waiting for an answer. When she comes back from the toilet, it is clear that she's been crying. She has been crying because she thinks that nobody listens to her and that she's a bad person. In other words, Katherine lives in a shadowy world and the only contact she has with reality is her alcoholic son, through tears and emotional suffering.

In order to put Katherine through therapy, I must first liberate her from her true sense of guilt towards her alcoholic son. The first two months of dialogue take the following form:

Katherine: I suffer so much. My poor son! One day he will die from his drinking (she starts crying).
Therapist: Yes, you're right to worry about him. You are a good mother. For, you have expressed your feelings for your poor son. But has he not been in therapy for his alcohol problem?
Katherine: Therapy? Who will be in therapy?
Therapist: No, no, not in therapy now, I ask if your son, Kris, has been in therapy in the past.
Katherine: My poor son! (She starts crying again) He has tried everything, but it has not worked. Why does my son suffer so much?
Therapist: What do you mean that he has done it all? He has been in therapy?
Katherine: Yes, yes, I cannot quite remember. He has been in therapy many times.
Therapist: Ah, ok, so now we are getting serious. Your son has been an alcoholic for the last 10 to 15 years and his future is dark and foggy.
Katherine: What future?
Therapist: Uh, excuse me, Madam Katherine, I'm not explaining myself. I would say that you have the right to suffer more than your son Kris, because he is an alcoholic. I agree with you.
Katherine: Ah! Hmm, ha-ha! I am very glad that you listen and understand me because the rest of my family is sarcastic towards me when I talk about Kris, so I cannot say anything to them.

Therapist: Uh, do you feel bad and suffer because you are afraid of Kris' abuse now and in the future, or you feel responsible because your son was already an alcoholic at the age of 15?
Katherine: I do not understand what you say, responsible to whom?
Therapist: Madam Katherine, I would like to know if you or your husband has discovered the reasons why Kris became an alcoholic. Have you any idea why he started drinking? What do the psychologists and psychiatrists have to say?
Katherine: All the psychologists and psychiatrists are such sweet and scientific people. They all make sense, but I cannot understand them when they talk to me.
Therapist: O.k., you're a good person with a good heart, Katherine. And your son is also a good person. But he can't stop drinking alcohol. In other words, we have still not understood why your son Kris became an alcoholic. Am I right?
Katherine: How can you know what is right? I do not understand you.
Therapist: All psychiatrists and psychologists are right, but they have not been able to find a way to help your son through therapy. That means, Katherine, it is not because of you or your husband that your son is an alcoholic. Or do you think maybe it was the way your husband treated your son, treating him badly and negatively, and that is the reason for your son's abuse?
Katherine: Yes, it's true that my husband can be very hard, but I do not know, for he is also very nice.
Therapist: So that means, Katherine, if you and your husband are not responsible for your son's abuse, then something else was. You won't help him by staying home and crying all day.
Katherine: But I feel terrible about the fact that my son suffers, so what else shall I do?
Therapist: If psychiatrists and psychologists can't help your son then you probably shouldn't take full responsibility of what needs to be done. You also have two other children. You must open your world a little and also see to your other two children.
Katherine: Well, my other children are doing well and have no use for me.

Therapist: Who says they do not need you? Have you asked them?
Katherine: You have said to me that they get annoyed when I talk about Kris. They push me out of their lives.
Therapist (Laughs): No, no, I'm not saying you should visit them and talk to them about Kris. I think you should just listen to them and open up your love towards them, the way you do with Kris.
Katherine: But I cannot be happy and laugh with them because my Kris feels bad and suffers.
Therapist: So if I understand you well, it is not so easy for you to be happy. You can't cry and at the same time open up and be happy.
Katherine: No, no, I can't be happy about anything in the world, even my husband. Everyone is sweet and tries to help me but I cannot be happy. I only think about Kris.
Therapist: So, if Kris is doing well, can you be happy - if he no longer has a drinking problem?
Katherine: So very happy, happy, happy… What do you think?
Therapist: I think if Kris is doing well you can be happy.
Katherine: No, unfortunately Kris will never be healed, I just know it.

This dialogue cannot continue because Katherine blames herself one hundred percent and has a very high guilty conscious. She does not suffer because Kris suffers, but tries to find a reason to suffer. Even if Kris gets well she will continue suffering constantly. Therefore it is necessary to stop this negative thinking. So I can proceed with therapy, it is necessary to put Kris in therapy parallel with Katherine in order to prove that her negative views have nothing to do with Kris. Her depression is her own. After a year of therapy Kris stops drinking alcohol and is healthy. As I expect though, Katherine is not able to see Kris' positive development. Katherine expects that Kris will start drinking again after about a year or two.

Dialogue therapy after one year

Therapist: Are you happy Katherine, because Kris is now healthy, happy and full of life?

Katherine: Yes, yes, I am, but I do not know how long he can keep it up.
Therapist: I can say that Kris will be healthy forever, he is healthy now and has been clean the last two months. Are you happy now?
Katherine: Yes, but I cannot be completely happy because I know that he will drink alcohol again.
Therapist: Who says so? How do you know that he will drink alcohol again?
Katherine: I cannot explain why, it's a feeling I have.
Therapist: Maybe you're right, but if I look at my track record with alcoholics, they stop drinking alcohol forever once they are finished with therapy.
Katherine. Yes, but Kris has been to many psychologists and continued drinking alcohol. Why should he not drink alcohol now and in the future?
Therapist: Katherine, Kris did not complete his therapy with other psychologists. He discontinued the therapy himself. With me he is completely finished. It is not because I'm smarter or better than the other psychologists, but because he went through all seven steps of therapy. Therefore I can say that he will not drink alcohol again. However, there is a 3 to 5 percent chance that he will drink alcohol again.
Katherine: See! You say yourself that there is a small chance.
Therapist: Good point Katherine, but the chances are miniscule. Shall we sit down and mourn everyday, waiting for Kris to become an alcoholic again? Shall we squander our lives that way? Should we never to go out on to the streets because we know that there is a psychopath out there? Shall we stay in and wait?
Katherine: No, you're right, but why can I not be happy?

I stop the dialogue here. Success! Katherine now understands her feelings of guilt towards Kris. We can now move on to her own guilt, which she already had as a child. Katherine no longer feels guilty about Kris, and she begins to tell me that there are some aspects of her husband that she dislikes. But she is not able to articulate exactly what aspects.

The therapy continues:

Katherine: For example, when my husband came home last night I was waiting by the door to show him a painting. When he saw it he told me that it was very beautiful and then walked past me and asked what we would have to eat.
Therapist: So what's the problem here?
Katherine: I don't know, but I started to cry because I felt he was very insensitive. I know that he was hungry because he came home from work, but could he not wait just five minutes and look at the painting that I had spent all day on. After all, it was a gift for him.
Therapist: Ah yes, now I understand. But is it not better for example, that you waited to show him the painting till after he'd eaten so he was satiated when he looked at it?
Katherine: My husband said the same thing. I know I'm a bad person doing the wrong thing all the time.
Therapist: Katherine, I cannot see why you're a bad person, but it is very obvious that you make a mistake here. You paint while your husband is working at his job and when he gets home he is hungry. Katherine, if a man is hungry his first instincts are that he must eat and then, with a full stomach, appreciate creativity. Can we agree here, Katherine?
Katherine: Yes, now I understand. I should have shown him the painting later.
Therapist: Yes, you make a mistake. It was wrong to show him your painting first. But have you hurt him - have you done something dangerous?
Katherine: No, no, I did not hurt him.
Therapist: O.k., so why do you feel so guilty?
Katherine: I do not know.

The kind of dialogue I was having after a year of therapy will teach the client to distinguish guilt from wrong. After 15 months of therapy Katherine learnt that failure is an evolutionary process and needn't be associated with guilt. After two years of therapy Katherine has learned where her guilty feelings came from and why she's felt like a bad person since she was five years old. Katherine's parents had a negative symbiosis and never expressed any love for each other. Katherine's mother was a strong and dominant matriarch in contrast to her father, who was weak and a perfectionist. He could not handle his mother's aggression and temperament. Therefore, by the time Katherine was five she already felt like she was at fault. She felt responsible for her parents not loving each other. Katherine's mother criticized her constantly and her father never stepped in to stop it. As an 18-year-old, when Katherine finished high school, she met her husband Peter who was studying to be an architect; he was just a poor student then. Katherine's mother did not like him for her own personal reasons and did not want Katherine to marry him. But when her father also disapproved of her relationship with Peter, things couldn't have been worse for Katherine. She felt guilty that she didn't listen to her father and marry a wealthy aristocrat. After Katherine's decision to marry Peter her mother almost completely cut off contact with her. When they did talk on the phone once or twice a year her mother made her feel guilty, as she herself didn't have a healthy relationship with her husband i.e. Katherine's father. But Katherine is lucky, because both her parents are alive and she has still has the opportunity to free herself from her guilt when she confronts them with her past.

6. Anders' therapy

Anders stopped teaching a at the school a year ago and has been on antidepressants since then. He lives alone in an apartment in downtown Copenhagen. When he comes in to see me he has not taken a bath in a long time and is not wearing clean clothes. I begin a dialogue with Anders to find out how he feels:

Therapist: How did you feel after you stopped working?

Anders: Not so good. I don't know how to explain it because I am an intelligent person.

Therapist: O.k. Anders, how is your sleep? Do you sleep well at night or wake up at about 5.00 am and then you can't sleep anymore?

Anders: No, no, quite the opposite. I go to bed at 5.00 am and then wake up at 1.00 or 2.00 pm

Therapist: So what do you do since you sleep so late - do you play computer games?

Anders: Yes I do, unfortunately I am completely dependent on my computer. But I'm not into pornography; I just play a war game.
Therapist (smiling slightly): Anders, why did you say that about watching porn? I know you are not watching porn, but why do you say that?
Anders: Because when I tell my friends that I sleep at five in the morning they tell me I should watch less porn.
Therapist: O.k., thank you for explaining it to me, but I'm not your friend but your therapist and I know you're not watching porn.

Anders doesn't ask me how I know this even though I say it very slowly and deliberately so there's no chance he couldn't have heard it. So I go on:

Therapist: So you stopped working Anders, because you go to bed at 5.00 am?
Anders: Umm, I, I don't understand you. What did you say?
Therapist (even slower): Anders, why did you stop teaching at the school?
Anders: Because I am depressed.
Therapist: Yes Anders, that's true, but the correct answer is that you go to bed at 5.00 am and cannot wake up again at 7.00 am.
Anders (gives me an uncomprehending look and leans in to stare as if I were an alien): Sorry, I do not understand you again.
Therapist (laughs slightly): Anders, I'm saying that you cannot wake up in the morning because you only sleep two hours a night. Therefore you cannot go to school.
Anders: Hmm, that way.
Therapist: Yes, Anders, it is necessary that you understand what you're doing in your life. Therefore I ask you these kinds of questions in the beginning. So Anders, what did you eat last night?
Anders (Looks at me as though it was the most difficult question in the world): Last night? (He thinks for a while but cannot answer)
Therapist: O.k., can you remember what day it was yesterday?
Anders: What day? (Again, very thoughtful)
Therapist: Yes, you know - Monday, Saturday or Tuesday?
Anders: (blank look)

Therapist: O.k. Anders, can you remember what day it is today?
Anders (laughs suddenly - like a sweet little schoolboy who has found the correct answer): Yes, yes, it's Wednesday today.
Therapist: How do you know that it is Wednesday today?
Anders: (Proudly gestures that he has written it in his calendar)
Therapist: Anders, congratulations! It is Wednesday today. So what day was it yesterday?
Anders: Hmm, in that way. Yes, I know now - yesterday was Tuesday.

But unfortunately Anders still cannot remember what he ate for dinner the day before. Anders's life has long been confined to playing computer games. He ate bread for dinner and he has not had any contact with reality. So for the first two months I practice natural, basic logic with Anders. For example:

Therapist: Anders, in which direction will the sun rise?
Anders (delighted): From the east.
I gave Anders the task of finding his way to a small village near Copenhagen without any maps, just by getting directions from people on the street. Anders ended up at a beach in Copenhagen and thought that he was in the village. He had been at the beach before but he was not sure that it was the village because it wasn't as far as I told him it would be (10-11 kilometers). He went no more than 3-4 kilometers away. I laugh as if Anders were an innocent and sweet child of about five years. I ask him:

Therapist: O.k. Anders, how can we find out where you've been?
Anders: I don't know. I'm not sure that it was the village.
Therapist: Did you meet any people when you were at the beach?
Anders (Glad): Ah yes, I see what you mean. So, I should have asked them where I was.
Therapist: Yes, but I'm completely certain you haven't been to the village Anders. What you described to me is a beach in Copenhagen, not a village.
Anders: Yes, maybe you're right. It was not 11 kilometers away, as you

said it would be, so why should it be the village – I just assumed it was. (But he never thought he should ask someone)

In the first two months of therapy, the innocent and sweet Anders learns to orient himself, to talk with people so he can find a village, to eat other things besides bread every night, to take a bath and to wash his clothes. We create a program that requires him to wake up each day at 11 am. From the 2nd to 5th month we work to free him from his guilt. For example, he shouldn't feel guilty about receiving social security. I explain that he shouldn't feel guilty for not working. He begins to take the train and travel 2-3 kilometer each day to go for a swim. Eventually he starts playing a little tennis every day, as he used to do. Anders starts to feel better as he uses his body. He begins to get in touch with old friends and because he now has an active life he begins to feel tired and sleep by one in the morning. Through various activities I wean Anders away from the computer. He begins reading the newspaper and his memory returns. After nine months I begin working with his real guilt that comes from his mother. His mother brought him up alone after his father's death when Anders was 10 years old. His mother did not help him when he needed support, but still had constant expectations of him. She burdened him with unnecessary and unearned guilt. For example, when Anders would come home in the evenings as a 13-14-year-old, she'd ask him why he'd been out playing with other boys and not home cooking for her. So Anders couldn't be social and play with the other boys because he felt guilty. He did little else except look after his mother and younger brother. Anders finally learned to distinguish between duties and guilt; he freed himself from his depression and after 12 months of therapy returned to the school to teach.

7. Pernille's therapy
Pernille cries constantly and feels very guilty about not continuing with her studies at the art academy where she was previously enrolled.
Dialogue therapy in the first two months:

Therapist: So, you stopped going to school because you couldn't concentrate on the readings or because things were just generally bad for you?
Pernille: I'm not sure. Both, I think.
Therapist: Yes, I can imagine, for they are related to one other. But if ask you today Pernille, to read one page of a book would you be able to do it and remember its basic meaning later?
Pernille: One page...hmm. What book will I be reading? (She begins crying)
Therapist: Any book you like. Which book would you like to read?
Pernille: I, I cannot read books right now. I feel very bad.
Therapist: I'm sorry, you're right - I've seen that you are very uncomfortable. But when you say bad do you mean it hurts in your head, chest or stomach - how do you suffer?
Pernille: I don't know. I'm not so good. (She is crying again)
Therapist: Uh, ok, let me ask you something else. When you get up in the morning, can you be out of bed before 10 am?
Pernille: Uh, no, no, I get up at 12 pm. Because I just can't get out of bed, I feel very bad. (She is crying again)
Now I pause while she drinks some water and wait until she is ready again.

Therapist: O.k., let's talk about something else. The period during which you stay awake, say between 12 and 5.00 pm, do you feel better or is it still bad?
Pernille: No, I'm alone and things are so bad that I can't even go out for groceries.
Therapist: O.k. does your mood change in the evening – do you feel like seeing some of your girlfriends?
Pernille: No, I only see my poor mother, who comes by with a little food for me. I feel so bad.

We take another short break and drink some water. After five minutes, when she is ready, I continue again:

Therapist: I'm sorry, but I need to ask you something to understand how exactly your depression came about. So, this was your first year at school?
Pernille: Yes
Therapist: Can you remember when it started how it developed into something so bad in your second year – was it just after Christmas? When you told me you thought you just had a cold and a little flu?
Pernille: I can't quite remember, but I think it had something to do with Christmas.
Therapist: Do you think that you were very disappointed with your parents at Christmas, because they hadn't acknowledged how hard you had worked so that the whole family could have a good Christmas?
Pernille: I can't remember. Perhaps yes, it had something to do with Christmas.
Therapist: For example, you spent over a month to find the perfect Christmas present for your parents? (She told me she'd visited many different stores). And you expected that they would be excited about their presents?
Pernille: Yes, I remember now. It is true. They just said thank you and then we continued unwrapping presents. (She begins crying again)
Therapist: But they expressed the same amount of excitement over your younger sister's (Marianne) present to them, even though she hadn't spent any time finding them a present?
Pernille: No, no, I also found a present from my sister to our parents. I had three options and just before Christmas Marianne selected one. It's the one I had suggested that she should give to our parents.
Therapist: Ah, ok, now I understand. Your sister spent only one day to find a present, because you had already done it all?
Pernille: To be honest, the worst part is the criticism from my sister. You have no idea how much she pushed me to find the right present. Many times I cried because I hate it when she scolds me and calls me a cow.
Therapist: So, have you told your parents that it was you who found the present they got from your sister?
Pernille: No, I must be very careful with her because she is very temperamental.

Therapist: Do you think Pernille, that you in a way are afraid of your sister?
Pernille: Yes, yes, maybe, I don't know.
Therapist: Uh, can you remember a little more from Christmas Eve? Sorry that I ask again, Pernille, because I know that you feel terrible about it, but it is necessary that I push you a little here.
Pernille: Yes, yes, it's ok, you may ask, I'll try to remember.
Therapist: Did you, for example, make a plan for when you should all sit down to eat, unwrap presents, decorate the Christmas tree and so on? And your family didn't follow the plan, so you were very disappointed and cried a little?
Pernille: Yes. I wept in the afternoon, it was terrible. And I also noticed that they were listening to everything Marianne suggested and not to me.
Therapist: Ok, no more questions about Christmas. But I understand you had a terrible Christmas and I can tell you that your depression started here, at this Christmas.
Pernille: I see! OKAY...okay (almost indistinct).
Therapist: So, after Christmas, it was impossible for you to concentrate on going about your daily tasks and you were put off the whole time!? And after April, therefore you had 3-4 big projects that you barely started!? And in May you were ill!? You started to cry, had a stomach ache and said you were sick!? It was impossible for you to cope with exams!? (All rhetorical questions) But why do you not want to start over?
Pernille: No, no, I can't. I stopped at the art academy because I did not know what to say to my fellow students.
Therapist: What do you think? Could you not say that you have been sick and now feel better again, because now it is July? And you have the option of being mentally well by September 1st, so therefore you can start school again.
Pernille: No, no, I know I will never get better. It ends with me.
Therapist: You're wrong. You are not my first client with depression, so I'm not experimenting with you. So, of course you will be healthy after a year and totally free from your depression. But I agree that right now you cannot start school again. Next September though, in about 14 months,

you will start in a new direction and with school; a new life.

My conclusion after two months of therapy is that Pernille cannot express her opinions to her parents and is afraid of her younger sister.

Dialogue therapy after 4 months
Pernille has had a girlfriend, Klara, since high school and she is afraid of her (the same way she is afraid of her younger sister):

Pernille: I do not know how to say this clearly because her boyfriend is my ex-boyfriend from a few years ago. I broke up with him a while ago. But every time I visit her and he's there, he hounds me and forces me into conversation with him. I don't like talking to him.
Therapist: So what do you do?
Pernille: I get totally confused and do not listen to what he says. I just say, "Yes, yes" to everything.
Therapist: So you compromise. In order to see your girlfriend you compromise. You pay such a high price just to see your girlfriend?
Pernille: But the worst thing part is that when the three of us are together, I'm forced to listen to all his idiotic talk about his successes at university, his excellent grades, how the others admire him and so on.
Therapist: Why do you call his talk idiotic Pernille?
Pernille: Because he only talks only about himself and the university and it is very, very boring. He never listens to Klara and me.
Therapist: Well said Pernille, it is true that he is a totally self-absorbed and boring person. But why don't you just meet Klara alone - without him?
Pernille: Yes, I've thought about that, but if I ask her out alone I might hurt her!?
Therapist: How can you hurt her, if you for example, invite her to the movies one night?
Pernille: Yes, but she never goes out without her boyfriend, Kim. And if I invite her out alone it means that I do not like him.
Therapist: Uh, not necessarily for, 1) you just want to be alone with her 2) what is wrong if you do not like him? He's Klara's boyfriend, not yours.

Pernille: Can you really tell someone that to their face?
Therapist (laughs): No, I don't think you should tell her. It is not your duty to tell her that you don't like her boyfriend, but try to distinguish your own ego from Klara's. If you do not like Kim, you are entitled to that because he is not your boyfriend and is also very self-centered. Conclusion: When you love your girlfriend Klara, it does not mean that you agree with all her choices. You can have a different opinion.
Pernille: I see! Now I understand it. I will not express my opinion about Kim to Klara, he is her choice and I must respect that. But I can see Klara alone and have fun with her.

After 9 months of therapy Pernille understood and accepted why she loves her father more than her mother - the opposite of what she thought at first. Pernille, as a little girl, used to go on holiday alone with her younger sister. Her father wouldn't give her any duties while on holiday - for example, having to take care of their grandparents or something. However, this was not true of her mother - when Pernille was seven years old, her mother made her travel to the south of Denmark together with Marianne, 100 kilometers away from their home in Copenhagen, to take care of their maternal grandmother. Pernille had depression when she was a 7 year old girl, stemming from guilt that she felt because apparently she had not done her duty (taking care of the grandmother). The guilt was exacerbated further when everyone would have a terrible time because her grandmother and younger sister quarreled all the time. Since then Pernille has protected her younger sister unconditionally. Therefore, she didn't even think of telling Marianne that she needs to find her own Christmas present for their parents. Pernille had started to understand all this.

Dialogue therapy continues:
Therapist: Why was it your responsibility to take care of your sister and maternal grandmother? Why?
Pernille: Because my mother told me that my grandmother was a bit of strange person who did not really take care of her when she was a child herself. And that's why she is also unable to express any love towards her

grandchildren – us.

Therapist: So Pernille, your mother is unable communicate with her mother. Why send you and your sister to her? Of course you would have a terrible time there.

Pernille: It was my nightmare. Every year I dreaded that time when we had to travel to the south. I knew my grandmother and sister would be arguing as usual and I would be crying every night.

Therapist: Have you ever told your mother what a tough ordeal this was for you as a little girl and that you couldn't be responsible for your grandmother?

Pernille: No, no, my grandmother also used to scold my mother over the phone. I remember seeing my mother keeping the phone instrument away from her ear when my grandmother was on the phone.

Therapist: O.k., so now you understand that the fault was completely your mothers. The question is why did your father not stop your mother from sending you down to your grandmother's?

Pernille: I know now. My father was weak and I thought he was strong.

Therapist: This is why you got depressed early in your life, Pernille. You took your parents' obligations on to yourself. And of course you felt guilty when your grandmother behaved badly.

Pernille completed her therapy in 14 months. She started to sets limits to her sister: she needed to buy her own presents and not be aggressive towards Pernille. She also showed her parents that they had committed a grave error, which is what started the depression. She started a new education in economics as scheduled, in September.

8. Mikkel's Therapy

Mikkel is an only child and his parents divorced when he was 17 years old. After the divorce, Mikkel's mother lived alone and did not find a new man. Mikkel's father moved to another town, married again and saw Mikkel once or twice a year after that. Mikkel had been noticing his parents' relationship deteriorate since he was ten years old. When Mikkel was 12 years old his parents had a big quarrel during which his father very loudly said that he wanted a divorce. The following day he told Mikkel about it. However, instead of getting a divorce, his parents stayed together for another five years without explaining to Mikkel how they resolved their differences. (It took nine months of therapy to make the client tell me this story)

Dialogue therapy in the first two months:

Mikkel (he breathes deeply and sighs): I'm not so good.

Therapist: Can you explain a bit more what you mean by that?

Mikkel: I am depressed, my girlfriend Birgit, tells me that I am very closed towards her and take no initiative. She is right. I feel so bad.

Therapist: Initiative towards what?

Mikkel: I don't know, but maybe she thinks that I don't talk that much. I don't challenge her enough.

Therapist: O.k., now I understand better. Can you, as an example describe to me what you do in the evenings?

Mikkel: Uh, nothing special. I come home, we eat some dinner, drink a little wine - nothing special.

Therapist: And afterwards?

Mikkel: I work a little on the computer to see if I have some email and maybe send a few to some friends. At about nine or ten, we watch some television together and then go to bed.

Therapist: How often do you have sex Mikkel?

Mikkel: One or two times a month... No, no, a week.

Therapist: How long have you been with your girlfriend?

Mikkel: Three months.

Therapist: Why did you choose to be with Birgit?

Mikkel: I don't know if I chose her, or whether it was more like she chose me - if I must be honest. (Laughs a little)

Therapist: But what did you do to get her attention?

Mikkel: Well, I've never thought much about why I chose to be with her because I am not so much into women. If I think about it, I'm not very experienced with women, because I've only had three women in my life.

Therapist: Do you mean three women you were in love with or just had

sex with?
Mikkel: I don't know if I was in love, but yes, I've only been with three women.
Therapist: Were they long or short relationships?
Mikkel: No, no, they weren't short but long relationships. They lasted two to three years and now I'm with a fourth woman.
Therapist: So, why did you end your relationship with these women - do you know?
Mikkel: Yes, of course. After a short while I lost interest in them.
Therapist: Ok, so do you think you left them or that they left you?
Mikkel: No, all three walked away from me, but I understand that they would not want to be with me because I had no interest in them.
Therapist: So why did you come to me today, Mikkel - what is your goal?
Mikkel: I am afraid that I have been depressed since my parents were divorced, because I don't feel so good about myself. I feel that I don't have real contact with the world and I have no energy or enthusiasm - except when I work.
Therapist: Ok, now I understand better why you decided to begin therapy Mikkel. You are afraid that you have been depressed since you were 17 years old. Also, a part of your depression is that you don't have the energy and desire to have transparent relationships with women or communicate with other people?
Mikkel: Yes, you are right. I'm in therapy now to take this depression away because the only time I feel well is when I am working.

After this dialogue where Mikkel says he feels something is missing and has no energy, I use two months to explain to Mikkel that he spent his childhood protecting a weak mother who was depressed and unable to work. As a child he was constantly looking for opportunities when his mother would say something and he could help her. He can't figure out how to take the initiative towards women because all the time he waits for them to say something so he can respond. For example, it never occurred to Mikkel that he could take a weekend trip with his girlfriend, or buy her flowers or take her out into the city. Everything for Mikkel has been a schedule. And if his girlfriend, for example, arranges a dinner with some friends that isn't part of the schedule it totally freezes Mikkel. He lacks the oversight to think about other people except himself. He excuses himself by saying that he has to work and then gets drunk when he comes home. Since he was a child he has been lonely and never learned to socialize with anyone apart from his parents because his parents never invited guests home - other than once or twice a year.

Therapy after 4 to 5 months

I give Mikkel the task is to travel with his girlfriend to London for four days. Mikkel organizes it all. He buys tickets, books a hotel and since his girlfriend is an artist, plans which museums they must visit, even though he is not so interested in art. They are even to go see a famous musical. My next meeting with Mikkel is after this holiday.

He comes in with a big smile and his body language has improved 100 percent – he is being himself and not playing any roles.

Therapist: Welcome back Mikkel. I look at you and see that you've changed completely.

Mikkel: Change?! This is not just a change! London was a great triumph for I am starting to experience my own feelings.

Therapist: Ah ha, ok. You are no longer in a bell jar, but outside.

Mikkel (in a voice coming all the way from the stomach): Yes! I know now that I've saved the gentleman in me. I don't quite know what happened to me (he spreads his arms in a questioning movement). When we were at the restaurant, I pulled my girlfriends' chair out for her. I do not know if it was the influence of the English way, but yes, I was a gentleman. And do you know what happened? For the first time, while I was out with my girlfriend, all I could think off is when we could back to the hotel and have sex. I noticed my sexual appetite. And we had sex every night. It was like waking up after a dark period where I had been hypnotized.

Therapist: Mikkel, you are starting to develop an ego. Congratulations! This is excellent, but I have a question for you - did you at any time during the four days feel like crying?

Mikkel: Yes! (With his left arm raised as a gesture of pride) I cried because I was so happy! I was in the bathroom and I cried because I was so happy.
Therapist: Mikkel, your tears were your liberation and you're crying because you were truly happy. Your emotions built up and just exploded in a good way and that is why you wept.

After 7 months of therapy Mikkel has renewed energy and starts being very proactive. He feels happy, well at work and enjoys being with his girlfriend. But he needs to understand his girlfriend more deeply.

Dialogue therapy after 7 months

Therapist: Mikkel, do you remember how you felt at school during the first three years, from the first to third grade, between the age of 7 to 9 years?
Mikkel: No, you know that I can't remember my past. I think I have said that to you. Therapist: Yes, that's true Mikkel, but today I will push you a little so you can begin to remember. For example, when you went to school did you come home and tell your mother how things were at school? Who you played with, what happened, etc.?
Mikkel: No, because it was my life and I felt fine at school. Why should I tell her?
Therapist: Is it that you think you did well at school and didn't need your mother's support...or that things weren't good for your mother at home so you didn't want to burden her with it because you were afraid that she could not handle it?
Mikkel: You're right, it was the second. There was a bad atmosphere at home and I felt good being in school. But up until now I thought that I did not need her support. But I'm beginning to understand that I was unconsciously protecting her.
Therapist: And now you remember how your relationship was with your father after this? You distanced yourself from him?
Mikkel: Funnily enough, I can't remember my father during those three years. Maybe he was not at home? I certainly cannot remember him being

a part of my life. Hmm...maybe he was busy working?

Therapist: That basically means, Mikkel, that when you finished school and came home you saw your mother alone and noticed her bad mood. What did you do?

Mikkel: Now I remember. I watched television for many hours - often until it was time to eat. Later, before I went off to sleep my father came and said good night and then I slept.

Therapist: What were you doing at home on weekends? Did you invite some friends home or visit your friends?

Mikkel: No, no, now I'm beginning to remember. I was alone and my father often took me fishing. Not every weekend, but sometimes. And we also went for a movie sometimes.

Therapist: Can you remember if you ever played with your father over the weekends - for example, handball, football or basketball?

Mikkel: No, no, my father never did any of that.

Therapist: O.k., can you remember if you every played with the other boys in your neighborhood or at school? Maybe football?

Mikkel: No, I didn't play with the other boys, because I always thought it was best to play with myself.

Therapist: O.k., Mikkel, can you understand now why you don't remember your past? You were not social, did not play with other children and were always alone.

Mikkel: Yes, but I did well by myself and had no use for others.

Therapist: Yes, but you pay a high price Mikkel, it is through others that we find out who we are. You have been missing that up until now Mikkel and that's you can't understand a woman's mind, build up friendships or have a family. You are 35 years old and still don't know if you want to get married and start a family!?

Mikkel: True. I have no friends and I haven't thought about getting married or having children. But is there something wrong with that?

Therapist: Mikkel, why can't you work all year round even though you love your job? It is not as you say, because you're tired of your job, but because you start to be aggressive towards your colleagues. You must first learn to manage them socially - not professionally. Secondly, when you

lose interest in a woman, you passively wait for her to leave you, instead of walking away from her yourself. But how was it for those last years when you were with them till they left you?
Mikkel: It was terrible, just terrible during those last years.
Therapist: So why didn't you just tell them?
Mikkel: Hmm, maybe because I was afraid that they would leave me.
Therapist: Yes Mikkel, you were afraid to express the experiences of your school life to your mother when you were a child because you were afraid that she would leave you too. As you can see, what you fear happens in reality. You were afraid to tell your girlfriends that you wanted to leave them and after two years they left you. Mikkel, you are no longer a child. Today we separate your childhood from Mikkel, the 35 year old adult. Children need to tell their parents about their world and from them learn about morals, ethics, boundaries and what is right or wrong. What you lacked as a child we will fix now and we will do it in practice. You must express your feelings, life and job experiences to your girlfriend and understand that a relationship is based on also sharing unpleasant things with one another. Your girlfriend is not your mother Mikkel, we can separate that. Your girlfriend will be very glad if you tell her about your problems at work. If you are lonely and don't talk about it to your girlfriends, then they cannot understand what is happening with you and therefore they leave you. You are not expressing anything to them and managing everything by yourself. This gives your girlfriends the impression that you have no space in your life for them and so they start maintaining a distance from you.

Dialogue after a year:
Mikkel has now understood that he needs to be proactive and express his feelings to his girlfriend, but when his girlfriend is in a bad mood herself, Mikkel is unable to keep his spirits up and gets into a bad mood himself.

Therapist: Mikkel, when your father left your mother, what did your mother say to you for the three years after the divorce?
Mikkel: She was angry because my father left us for another woman who

he married and is still married to. And I was also very angry with my father. I hated him.
Therapist: Why do you hate your father? Because he left your mother? What was the right thing to do? Should he be with your depressed mother although he is not happy being with her? For her sake or for yours?
Mikkel: Hmm, I've never thought about it because I was alone and I just protected my mother – she wept for three years.
Therapist: Mikkel, I understand your feelings and you're right - you love your mother. But was your father was responsible for your mother's depression? Or was your mother depressed even before she met your father?
Mikkel: I don't know. It was just three tough years. When I was 12 years old, deep inside me I wished that they'd separate because my father shouted for my mother. Things like, 'Why can't you work a little more and earn some more money?' But what happened later was a total disaster. I was alone, had to cope with high school, had a depressed mother and when she wept, I wept with her.
Therapist: Mikkel let me summarize here - as a child between ten and twelve years you wished that your father would disappear, because he treated your mother badly. But since it happened when you were seventeen, it was a disaster and life still wasn't any better. Am I right?
Mikkel: That's right. It was a disaster. And it was not just the three years. Even when I moved out, I continued to protect and look after her two or three times a week.
Therapist: Do you shout at your mother or scold her, they way your father used to?
Mikkel: NO, no! Never! I take care of her and am very sweet to her.
Therapist: So, is she better now because you are sweet to her? Has she changed or is she psychologically unchanged?
Mikkel: Unfortunately, she is the same. After my father left us my mother got worse. She has never had a new man or friends in her life. She is unable to open up.
Therapist: So, this means that things didn't get harder for your mother because your father left her but because she is depressed!? And that's why

you can't help her, even if you do the opposite of what your father did - even if you are very sweet and careful.

Mikkel: Now I see what you mean. My father left my mother because he could not help with her depression.

Therapist: Yes Mikkel, but here's how it has affected you: When your girlfriend feels low, you don't say anything to her because that's the way you've handled your mother, but it didn't help her. The difference is that your girlfriend is not depressed and needs you to say things to her because you have an overview and an opinion - and she will react differently from your mother. Instead of blocking out and losing your good humor as you did with your mother, show it to your girlfriend and express your opinion.

Mikkel has the right to be aggressive towards his father because the father has not explained to him why he left his mother. Not to point out faults in his mother but quite the contrary, for Mikkel's own sake.

After 14 months of therapy

Mikkel confronts his father and hears his father's version of the story - his father couldn't cope with his mother and it affected his job - he lost money, the house they owned and suddenly couldn't take anymore. He began to be depressed himself and therefore decided to divorce the mother. He admitted that he made a big mistake because it has obviously affected Mikkel very much. Mikkel explains to his mother that he can't take care of her anymore and she needs professional help. She shouldn't call him every weekend and expect him to come visit her because she doesn't feel good because he needs to build his own personal life, girlfriend, family and children. He visits her whenever he wants - for his sake and not hers. Therapy is finished.

9. Torben's therapy

When Torben comes in he is thin and has long hair - like an old hippie from the seventies. When he speaks his body language shows that he is tired.

Torben (makes a face and tilts his head slightly): I'm not so well, I've been depressed for ten years now - and my doctor says my dose of happy pills is up. I don't like that. I've been to a psychiatrist and psychologist for ten years now, but instead of getting better, I just got divorced again (with a painful expression).
Therapist: So what do you want from me Torben? What can I do for you?
Torben: I want my wife, Isabella back.
Therapist (smiling): Uh, I cannot promise you that. But I can help you to understand what happened, why your wife left you and maybe create some opportunities so you can get her back.
Torben: But I know already why she left me.
Therapist (laughing): O.k., so since you already know tell me why she left you.
Torben: Because I have no permanent job and lack structure in my life. But I am an artist! I cannot live any other way. When I want to paint, I paint all night and sleep at eight or nine o'clock in the morning.
Therapist: O.k., thank you Torben, now I understand. What does she do?
Torben: Not a damn thing.
Therapist: Excuse me?
Torben: She is a trained architect but has never had a job.
Therapist: O.k., so you both have no jobs and get social security from the government?
Torben: Yes, in a way, because I work too little. So I earn very little.
Therapist: O.k., now that I understand your life I can ask you this - why did you separate?
Torben (grimaces with his eyes closed): Because... she said to me that I need to get up in the morning to look after our thee children and take them to kindergarten.
Therapist: So she left you?
Torben: Not just that, but uh, we had no money and I have no interest in going on holidays in the summer and such - but she insisted. Nor can I ah... stand her parents - very conservative and stubborn people. And we fought a lot, Isabella and me. Therapist: When you say fought do you mean physical or just verbal - with words?

Torben: No, no, not physically - only verbally. But uh... one or two times she has actually hit me - now I remember.
Therapist: And how did you react when she hit you, did you as a reflex hit back?
Torben: No, no, not in the slightest - it is not my style to beat, especially not women. I do not like to fight.
Therapist: How long were you together before Isabella left you?
Torben: Four, five years. I can't quite remember. Now she has a psychopath boyfriend and doesn't let me see my children. I may not get them this weekend. And when I insist, she threatens to go to court and get full custody because I'm a bad father.
Therapist: Torben it's a complicated situation but I must ask - why do you want to get her back? Do you want to change your life and have a different lifestyle or are you just afraid to be alone without a wife and children?
Torben: I love her and I'm not afraid to be alone.
Therapist: Torben how can you say that you love her when you have lived together for three or four years, quarrelling constantly and not changed anything for her?
Torben: Well...is it not because of love that we quarrel?
Therapist: No, because when we quarrel, we try to get a solution to a problem instead of arguing over the same problem. That is not love but a state. I will live in my own world and not communicate. But Torben you said you are depressed. Why do you think so? How are you depressed?
Torben: I have no energy in the mornings, as I said I couldn't even take the children to kindergarten. When I picked them up from kindergarten I had no energy. I needed to build a positive atmosphere at home. There was a bad vibe.
Therapist: Torben, it's not about you wanting Isabella back, but about how you, as you say, can build a positive atmosphere at home and be happy; to have structure in life and a normal father's relationship with your children, to move forward in life as a winner. Because if I ask you whether you feel like a winner or a loser, what would you say to me?
Torben: I, I, I am a loser. Not because I do not feel good myself, but because people do not understand my feelings - I am very sensitive. For

example, I am a big nature person so if I, for example, see a wounded animal it upsets me very much.
Therapist: Wonderful Torben, congratulations! You really are a good person. In therapy you must learn to express the same feeling you have towards animals to humans as well. But remember that you are in therapy so you shouldn't hide anything from me - that will not serve you well. In therapy you learn not only to be sensitive, but also how to deal with other people's opinions without getting hurt.

Is Torben really depressed?

George's Therapy
George is 45 years and has been especially aggressive the last two months. Last month he found out that he is depressed

Dialogue the first two months:
George (in a deep voice): I am very tired of... my wife... my children... all people. And I don't know... I cannot cope with human stupidity. It makes me crazy and then I'm aggressive. I argue with them and then close myself up in my own world. And you know what? I can't help it. I have made the same mistakes over the last twenty years (in a higher voice) again, again, again... I need to shut up when I'm stupid (thumps the table).
Therapist: What do you need from me, George? You are a smart man.
George: I don't know... no, no, I know. I need an explanation of why I make the same mistakes again and again. And the worst part is that all the idiots who provoke me think they are right! They cannot understand what big fucking idiots they are!
Therapist: And uh, you're trying to help them understand their mistake, am I right?
George: Yes, exactly (again with a loud voice).
Therapist: And maybe you are aggressive about the fact that they do not understand you and you provoke them with irony and sarcasm when you try to explain things to them?
George: Yes, exactly! It is true. O.k.! (Spread his arms) I have finally found

a man who understands me.
Therapist: Thank you for the compliment, George. I don't know if I'm on the same level as you but I'll try at least to understand you without provoking sarcasm or irony. That's a promise. But George, I have a question for you. Do you what Pythagoras, the Greek philosopher and father of mathematics, said about pearls and pigs? We do not throw pearls to pigs because they eat them.
George (pointing with his right hand): Yes, that is true. I throw my pearls to pigs! (Stands up suddenly and starts to walk around)
Therapist: Maybe it's an explanation of why you are aggressive - because you're trying to help people socially beneath you.

For the first two months of therapy George was very enthusiastic and answered thousands of questions about his personal life to show how good he is and how well he deals with stupid people. He is lonely and has no friends because he pushes them out of his life. He provokes unaware and illiterate people to be against him. He lives in a fantasy world as a modern Don Quixote (by Cervantes), but only without Quixote's assistant Pancho and the princess Dulcinea. George fights the whole world alone, wants to help and change everyone and this is why he is almost manic. Many of his ideas are good but the way he expresses them is fundamentally wrong because he degrades all human beings and has no respect for anyone except himself. It is therefore impossible for other people to be around George for more than half an hour at a time and George is to a certain degree aware of this. Therefore, for the last 10 years he has been aggressive all day every day without anyone listening to him.

Is George's manic-aggressive behavior a manic-depression or not?

These were 10 examples of therapy as per the Sisifos method, all related to depression or partly to depression. Let us now have a look at two other forms of therapy used to treat depressed people. The first is the Freudian model, which we today call psychodynamic psychotherapy, and the second is cognitive therapy for depression.

Psychodynamic therapy

The dominant position when it comes to psychotherapy of major depressive states (formerly called endogenous depression) is that it may be harmful and even dangerous to engage in psychotherapy in this area.

Freud defined the psyche as an energy system based on the assumption that early childhood events impact the further development in human beings, which means that the earliest events and experiences leave permanent traces on the human psyche. For example; an inborn vulnerability will make that person particularly sensitive to certain experiences. Early experiences are vital because they build basic trust or mistrust and harmonious or inharmonious personal development. In 1917 Freud wrote that 'Loss is central to an understanding of all forms of depression.' When we talk about loss in the psycho-dynamic sense, it may refer to the death of a spouse, loss of one's job, injury or disappointment.

According to Melanie Klein, who has worked extensively with Freudian theory, everyone goes through a depressive phase early in life. The depressive state begins as early as five or six months, when the child begins to experience that the good and the bad mother are one and the same person and that it both loves and hates the mother. The child's natural aggression towards the mother, cannot be interpreted or expressed and causes the child to think that expressing it will kill the mother. This fear automatically creates a sense of guilt because the child is dependent on the mother. Guilt is necessary to a certain degree for normal development (only psychopaths feel no guilt), but excessive levels of guilt are debilitating. The conflict between love and hate builds a psychological immune mechanism in the child that it uses to defend itself. This mechanism has two different forms. The first is a 'repair' mechanism. The child thinks it has caused the mother to die when she is not present and accordingly caused her to live when she resurfaces. The repair consists of impulses to make amends, love and care for the mother. Gradually however, the child realizes that its emotions and impulses can neither kill nor make the mother live, and it learns to deal with conflicting emotions without much anxiety, thus recognizing that others as well as the child itself are both good and bad.

The second type of immune mechanism is manic 'defense', which is a denial of dependence and guilt towards the mother and the related depression, and thus freedom of the child from the fear of harming the person it loves most.
The preceding hypotheses are very difficult to accept, although they do offer explanations of the human psyche, they are ultimately just guesswork as there is no way to know whether the baby, as proposed in Melanie Klein's theory, can accommodate all the ideas that she attaches to babyhood. However, when we conduct therapy, we can see if all this is really true. Therapy makes it very apparent that depressed people have feelings of guilt. Moreover, in line with Klein's theory, depressed babies feel bad when their parents feel bad. But when parents change moods and feel happy, contrary to Klein's theory, depressed babies only feel worse because they believe that the parents are play acting for their sake. This means that depressed people become aggressive themselves because they believe that they are the only ones who can see through their parents' role play. This is a paranoid and manic logic and proof that depressed clients do not, as Melanie Klein's theory states, combine two pictures (good and bad) into one.

Therefore it is also more logical and sensible to accept Aristotle's theory as written in his first book on the psyche. According to Aristotle human beings develop their senses first through hearing and then through pictures. Furthermore, while it is very important that a child's senses are developed through pictures, it must be noted that babies cannot understand their true meaning. The act of putting pictures together is for the child to experience. Bringing many similar experiences together creates an image or association for the child. An experience is what may lead a young boy to feel attracted to the color red and the smell of roses. This is an experience that he remembers and puts into his memory, along with many other pictures, after which he does not give it any more thought. When this boy is 15 or 16 years old and sees a beautiful girl, the image or perception of the rose will automatically kick in. He'll tell the girl that she looks and smells like a rose. In other words children do not think and feel as much as Melanie Klein proposes they do. Children up to their 4th year are totally dependent on their mother's ego and experience the world through their mother's vision of the world. This also explains why children cry when their mother is not around them. They don't understand that their mother may need to go to the toilet but automatically assume that they've been left alone in the world. Not, as Melanie Klein says, because they think they have killed their mother.

Children's experiences and pictorial development is also evident when children play mind games like 'memory' or guessing games. In these games, they often win over adults because they can connect more pictures than adults and remember them with their photographic memory, while adults try to assemble images using logic. The conclusion is that children until their 5th year live in a fantasy world in which they don't really think and cannot distinguish between fantasy and reality. They use their mother and later their father to understand the world's reality.

To pick up on a previous note, one can easily start psychotherapy with a client in the depressive phase, but first and foremost it is important to establish a relationship with the client showing interest, care and empathy. Listen to what the client has to say and make it clear that the feelings of extreme guilt and self-blame are unjustified. The conscience of depressed patient's - their 'super-ego' in Freudian terms - is especially cruel, stubborn and specific to the severely depressed. This can be explained through the overdeveloped ego of the depressive, full of anger that the client cannot express, causing strong internal self-condemnation. If successful therapy helps unleash some of this anger, the depressed do not judge themselves so harshly and their self-esteem improves, which ultimately leads to a release from close dependence on others and less vulnerability. The aim of therapy is to create a development and awareness in the client that changes on the way they discover and understand themselves and the world, over time preventing fresh depressive periods.

Cognitive therapy

Cognitive therapy is a form of therapy comparable to psychotherapy, using interviews as a method to recover from mental illness. In cognitive therapy, perceived thinking (cognition) is a critical part of mental illness, which is why a change in thinking is central to the therapeutic conversation. Cognitive therapy provides insights that can be used to improve a client's ability to process current problems by thinking in nuanced, rational and self-supportive ways. A central concept in cognitive therapy is automatic thoughts i.e. thoughts that arise quickly, instinctively and are experienced as the truth about a situation. Depressive thinking often gives rise to disparaging and pessimistic thoughts like, 'I'm good for nothing', 'Nobody cares about me' and 'The future is hopeless.' Such thoughts are examples of habitual negative thoughts, which among other things encourage depression, make the person lose faith in themselves and lose hope that their depression will ever go away. Negative habitual thoughts thus create a vicious circle that maintain and exacerbate a depression.

Besides the negative, automatic emotion is the cognitive therapeutic approach more fundamental and non-conscious personality traits called 'skemata', which is the term for the cognitive structures that allow an impression to be experienced and evaluated in ways that are meaningful to the person themselves. Skemata develop through a person's interactions, life conditions, environment and basic self-perceptions. An example of such a self-perception in a depressed person would be, 'I'm not perfect so that means I'm a failure.' During a depression positive skemata will be suppressed and negative schemata will dominate (the circle).

Let's have a look at why these two therapy methods can prevent effective therapy. Perhaps it is because they cannot diagnose major depressive disorder (moderate to severe depression). Perhaps it is because they confuse depression with depressive phases stemming from other symptoms. Therefore, it is necessary to understand the basis on which these methods diagnose depression. Over the past 50 years these models have been developed with the aim of helping doctors understand patients with both physical and psychological depressive symptoms.

Question: Are these questionnaires specific to a therapy method (such as cognitive and psychodynamic therapy), or are they just general questionnaires designed to (among other things to help doctors) diagnose major depressive disorder?

1. WHO questionnaire on wellbeing

The questionnaire below is based on Zunge's depression scale and the original contains ten questions, but we have only included five below. The scoring system is based on the fact that patients who score 0 to 1 in questions 4 and 5 have a high probability of having depression.

The following five questions assess how you have been feeling the last two weeks. Please circle the number next to each question that best describes your state. A higher score means a better wellbeing.

	How often do you:	All the time	More than 50% of the time	Less than 50% of the time	At no time
1.	Feel calm and relaxed?	3	2	1	0
2.	Feel full of energy?	3	2	1	0
3.	Wake up feeling fresh and well rested?	3	2	1	0
4.	Is your life busy and full with activities that interest you?	3	2	1	0
5.	Feel sad and low?	0	1	2	3

Sum of all answers from 1 to 5:

If the total is less than 5 you should contact your doctor.

3. GHQ-questionnaire

Besides this questionnaire there is also the GHQ questionnaire (Goldberg's General Health Questionnaire). It contains questions that are a combination of life quality and depression issues. The questions assess the probability of a person developing depression and a part of the questionnaire needs to be answered by a family member (as studies show that depressive people are often unable to accurately assess their own condition). The questionnaire only collects information about the past two weeks, because according to Goldberg, depressed patients do not have a long term memory.

Please answer the following 12 questions based on how accurately they assess your state over a period of the past two weeks. Please circle a score next to each question that best describes your condition. A higher score means a better wellbeing.

Have you or the family member in question:		Yes, completely	Mostly	To a certain extent	Not at all
1.	Been completely healthy?	3	2	1	0
2.	Been able to concentrate on what he / she has been doing?	3	2	1	0
3.	Felt full of energy?	3	2	1	0
4.	Kept yourself occupied?	3	2	1	0
5.	Had a tendency to lose interest in everyday tasks/chores?	0	1	2	3
6.	Overall felt that you are feeling well?	3	2	1	0
7.	Pleased with the way you go about doing things?	3	2	1	0
8.	Expressed any warmth or affection towards you?	3	2	1	0
9.	Believes that he/she matters to the surroundings and plays a role?	3	2	1	0
10.	Been able to take decisions?	3	2	1	0

11.	Seems to enjoy daily life?	3	2	1	0
12.	All things considered been happy?	3	2	1	0

Sum of all answers from 1 to 12:

If the total is less than 12 one should contact a doctor.

3. Major Depression

A third major depression questionnaire contains the 10 important indicators that the physician takes into account to make a 'major depression' diagnosis. It is this diagnosis that the Board of Health requires to be presented when the physician recommends the use of antidepressants.

Please answer the following 12 questions based on how accurately they assess the person's state over a period of the past two weeks.
The table below is divided into two columns that list three possible answers on each side.
If five or more answers are checked in the first column then therapy for (major) depression is required.

How often do you: (mark with a cross)	All the time	Most of the time	More than 50% of the time	Less than 50% of the time	Almost never	Never
1. Feel sad and sorry?	---	---	---	---	---	---
2. Lose interest in daily tasks and activities?	---	---	---	---	---	---
3. Feel you've lost your energy and drive?	---	---	---	---	---	---
4. Feel a lack of self confidence?	---	---	---	---	---	---
5. Have a bad conscious or feel guilty?	---	---	---	---	---	---
6. Feel that life is not worth living?	---	---	---	---	---	---
7. Find it difficult to concentrate on simple tasks like watching television or reading the newspaper?	---	---	---	---	---	---
8. Feel very tired or that things are moving too slowly?	---	---	---	---	---	---

9.	Have trouble sleeping at night?	---	---	---	---	---	---
10.	Experienced a loss of appetite or felt you've lost weight?	---	---	---	---	---	---

Questions asked in the Sisifos Method

The Sisifos method does not use a fixed questionnaire because if we pose open-ended questions as it is done in the other questionnaires, clients will answer 'always' to everything, but this cannot be true. If this were reality, they would feel deep pain and constantly be in the black zone and we know that there really are only two black zone periods - at 40 days and 6 months. Instead, the following are illustrative of the kind of questions we ask clients to diagnose depressive symptoms rather than simply classify them as depressed or not.

	How often do you: (mark with a cross)	Never	More than or about half the time	Always
1.	Find it difficult to concentrate on simple tasks like watching television or reading the newspaper?	---	---	---
2.	Get up late in the night at say 3.00 am and then again early in the morning at say 5.30 am?	---	---	---
3.	Can you get out of bed by 9.00 am?	---	---	---
4.	Have the energy to handle your chores the days you get out bed before 9.00 am?	---	---	---
5.	Feel that life is not worth living?	---	---	---
6.	Have a bad conscious or feel guilty?	---	---	---
7.	Think about committing suicide when you feel physical pain in your body (like a pneumonia)?	---	---	---

If the client's response to questions 3, 4 and 6 is 'more than half the time' then they have classical major depression, as only depressed people respond to these questions. If they are not depressed, they would answer 'never' to all three questions. If their response to question 7 is 'more than half the time' then they have manic depression.

Comments

1) In the 10 examples of dialogue therapy cited earlier in the book, I did not ask the clients questions 2, 3 and 7

2) Furthermore in these examples, as a therapist I worked with the clients in seven or eight different ways. If all of them were depressed then in principle I should have worked with them using the same tactics or approach. Why did I not do so? Perhaps because only five of the ten were examples of therapy for depression, the remaining were other symptoms or a bout of depression induced by another symptom. So what were these five other examples if not depression? I can help by citing the five symptoms most likely to be confused with depression: melancholy, martyr, borderline, narcissism and marijuana abuse.

3) In all ten examples we start with the clients' current life situation and towards the end of therapy reveal the cause of their symptoms (for example, aggressive parents, divorced parents, immature parents, lack of parents etc.). Therefore, in theory we could say that the Sisifos method is a combination of cognitive and psychodynamic therapy. The psychodynamic model focuses on the past and cause of the symptom, so I didn't reveal the cause of the symptoms in the 10 examples. I did not present the hidden causes which were responsible for clients' symptom, which I will do now.

1. The hidden causes for Maria's symptom

Maria disappointed her father because she wasn't as strong as him, for example; to be able to say to her classmates that maybe communism is right and capitalism is wrong. Since Maria didn't have her father's ability to defend herself, she became a victim of the class. As a victim she goes on in life to pick a husband like Petro, who is not a communist, because she inversely believes does not deserve to be with a man who is strong or like her communist father who she idolized. But Maria was in fact also a victim of the civil war and her father was far from a perfect God. When Maria was a little girl he was in jail, unable to protect his daughter and take an active and educational role in her life. It was Maria's father who made a mistake by creating false impressions of the war in Maria's mind.

Therapy taught Maria how to, among other things, confront her father and realize it is not she but her father who is a victim of the war. She also learns how to distinguish her own ego from her father's - communism was his ideology not hers. Maria also starts to look up to her mother, who raised her alone and overcame the challenges that a single mother with a husband in prison faces. When Mary realizes all of this she gets her freedom. Her liberation teaches her to put things in perspective - her mother was a real winner and her father a poor victim.

2. The hidden causes of Elleni's symptom

Elleni is unable to picture her father as a negative and vicious person, because children are unable to accept that it is possible that their father does not love them. Since Elleni's father beat her as a child, she simply believed he was entitled to do so because she had done some things wrong and was feeling guilty. This feeling grew with her and that's why she still feels the same way now as a 30 year old. Her mental image of her father (as a psychopath) doesn't enable her to maintain a distance from him, on the contrary - she tries constantly to get recognition from him. Because of this ambivalent relationship with her father, she has not yet been able to accept a man into her life, which means that she is locked into the fantasy world of a five-year girl. For her love is synonymous with weakness and she reacts in a way masculine way by placing herself in a patriarchal role. She thinks that violence and aggression are the right way, even though she dislikes it.

Elleni's masculine identity drives her to constantly push limits, explaining why she was the victim of two rapes, which she kept a secret. But these two episodes just contributed to her self-perception of being a bad person since her father had the right to beat her. This also contributed to her being constantly unfaithful and not wanting to be in a steady relationship with a man. In her fantasy world she fights all decent and good men to liberate herself from her crazy father, which ultimately only reinforces her idolization of him. This symptom is the most dangerous in therapy since a client with this symptom keeps reality very well hidden and projects their fantasy to be reality. What Elleni calls rape, for example, was only a half truth. In both cases she provoked sex by walking around naked in front of the men who 'raped' her. When the men responded by trying to kiss her, she even kissed them back but said, 'Let's just kiss a little, I don't feel like anything beyond that.' Despite this they went on to have sex in which she participated willingly. However, this reality became rape because she decided it would be. Elleni has forgotten that she had an active role in the encounters and even provoked them by prancing around naked.

Another possibility is that these encounters never occurred. It is just Elleni's need to have some kind of revenge against men because she doesn't like men. She plays her role as a victim to the letter by putting on a perfect exterior, making it very difficult for people to see her inner truth.

Therapy for this kind of symptom is very intense from start to finish. Elleni freed herself by confronting her father. She told him that she thinks is a monster and making it clear that if in the future she ever sees her mother bruised again, she will report him to police.

3. The hidden causes of Sofia's symptom

Sofia lived a life where her uncle's dog got more love than her. She has no self confidence and believes that her mother is responsible for the terrible life Sofia had because her mother left it to her sister to bring up Sofia. Since Sofia is unable to express her hatred for her mother she is mentally blocked. This blockage means that she, when her ex-husband beat her, felt she deserved it because she feels guilty and deserves punishment. When Sofia understands that her mother actually saved her life by leaving her to her sister, she is able to forgive her mother and liberate herself from her symptom. In the end Sofia truly believed that her mother handed Sofia over to her sister because she loved her daughter.

4. The hidden causes of Julia's symptoms

Her whole life Julia has denied that her father suffered from a psychosis and that her mother was totally passive. So she grew up in an environment where she, among other things, was bullied at school. At 19 she gets pregnant with a soldier who then leaves her alone with their daughter. Since Julia has never expressed her hatred and aggression towards her father, she now sees an opportunity to express it towards her absent husband. She built up a fantasy that she'd fallen in love with him and does not understand why he left her (although they were together only once). She contradicts herself by pointing out that he was too young to be a father. This makes Julia compete with her daughter and blame her for her father's disappearance. When Julia's daughter eventually has her own boyfriends and they quarrel, Julia sides with the boyfriends and never her daughter. Through therapy we make these different relationships clear to Julia. She sees this reality, expresses and accepts her hatred for her psychotic father and she frees herself from her symptoms (not completely though because her father is no longer alive).

5. The hidden causes of Katherine's symptom

Katherine's mother never really cared for her and always judged her. Her father never set limits for her mother. As a result Katherine would constantly feel guilty about never being able to do anything right. When she marries a (strong-willed) man her mother feels jealous and opposes the match. Katherine does not listen to her mother and goes ahead with the marriage, consequently feeling even guiltier because her parents now start maintaining a distance from her. This means she is constantly in doubt about her choice. She questions her marriage and questions herself – should I have listened to my mother? In reality, she feels sad that she could not (once again) satisfy her mother with her life choices. She starts provoking her husband by constantly opposing him without explaining why, so he can constantly berate her. For example, she buys very cheap and ugly clothes although she gets a lot of money from her husband. When he asks her why she does this, she gives examples like - the children in Africa do not have proper clothing. He reacts by donating to

African charity funds but she continues to buy ugly clothing. Or she will buy very expensive designer clothes for her daughter but nothing for herself because she can make do with her old clothes. Katherine frees herself when she expresses her aggression towards her mother, which automatically results in her ceasing to provoke her husband and compete with her daughter.

6. The hidden causes of Anders' symptom

Anders' mother hid from him the fact that his father left her when Anders was 10 years old. She has always given Anders the explanation that his father was sick and that was why he did not live with them. She did not explain why he was sick and the nature of the sickness. As a 12 year old Anders meets his sick father who does not offer any explanation for his absence either. When Anders is 16 his father dies and Anders finally learns that his father was a substance addict.

Anders had never expressed the aggression stemming from his mother's half-explanation and his father's complete lack of explanation. Once he understands how much the lack of protection from his father and nurturing from his mother has affected him, Anders discovers his right to be aggressive instead of feeling guilty. In the process he frees himself from his symptom.

7. The hidden causes of Pernille's symptom

When Pernille understands and expresses that it was not her but her mother's responsibility to take care of her grandmother, and that it was her father's obligation to not allow so much responsibility to fall on his five-year old daughter's shoulders, Pernille frees herself from her guilt and symptom.

8. The hidden causes of Mikkel's symptom

As a 14-15 year old Mikkel wished that his father, who was treating his mother badly, would leave her so Mikkel could take care of her himself. Mikkel realizes after the divorce though that he cannot help his mother.

As a result he develops a bad conscience and feelings of guilt. As Mikkel's mother continues to feel lonely and miserable when Mikkel leaves home, Mikkel cannot open up his own feelings to any other woman. The omnipresent guilt ensures Mikkel will not be able to take care of a woman at all. Mikkel believes God is punishing him for when he, as a 12 year old boy, prayed that his father would leave home. In an illogical way Mikkel thinks that God answered his prayers when his father left his mother. But when his father left things got even worse for his mother so Mikkel started to believe he was responsible for destroying his mother's life. This is why he is completely passive and cannot share his world with any woman. When Mikkel understands that children are not accountable for their parent's reactions and that he has been trapped in his Oedipus complex he frees
himself of his symptoms and finishes therapy.

9. The hidden causes of Torben's symptom

Torben is a divorced child who lived alone with his mother since he was four years old. At some point his mother marries again, this time a good but weak man who lets her take all the decisions. The mother does not want her new husband to be a part of Torben's upbringing. So, Torben grows up without a father (his biological father disappears completely after the divorce) and even the role his stepfather could have played. Torben is brought up by his strong mother alone and therefore believes a girlfriend also needs to take care of him the same way. Through therapy Torben realizes that every boy, besides his mother's love, also needs a masculine parental figure. He frees himself of his symptom and finishes therapy.

10. The hidden causes of George's symptom

George had a rich and successful father who was never home; his mother was a housewife, dependent on her husband's money and she spent her time waiting for her husband to come home. George hated his mother's dependence on his father – he saw his mother as his father's servant. He loves his mother because she was always with him and hates his father because he was never home. He has never seen his mother set limits for his father, for example by insisting that George needs a father and so he should be home more often. As a result, for George it became natural that a father should never be home. Moreover, by virtue of always being with her mother, George develops many feminine traits, never plays with other boys or has limits set by his father. In therapy George understands that his father made a huge mistake by not being home and letting his wife play a dual role and that George needs to express his gratitude towards her. He frees himself from his symptom and finishes therapy.

THE PSYCHOANALYSIS AND PSYKOSYNTHESIS OF DEPRESSED PEOPLE

	Psychoanalysis (elements)		**Psychosynthesis (characteristics)**
1.	Pain	→	Negative self image (feeling physically and mentally ill)
2.	General phobias	→	Hopelessness
3.	Suspicion and doubt – unable to trust anyone	→	Guilty conscious
4.	Constant stress and anxiety	→	. Lack of or no instinctive feels (hunger, thirst, sex)
5.	Constant confusion	→	No concentration abilities
6.	The black zone	→	No communication with the outside world, total seclusion
7.	Paranoia & Hypochondria, building a fantasy world	→	Self inflicted torture, suicide

The table above describes the seven basic elements of psychoanalysis, each of which corresponds to seven fundamental characteristics in psychosynthesis.

Let's see how the elements work and what results they produce, for example; pain, both physical and psychological, is considered to be the first element in psychoanalysis. Physical pain means actual pain in the muscles or a pneumonia-like feeling in the entire body. Psychological pain is, amongst many other things, caused by major events like the death of a loved one, a divorce or being fired from one's job. These forms of pain lead to a negative self image – the feelings of being a bad person - which if left to runs its course can ultimately lead to the 'black zone'.

This first fundamental characteristic leads to the second element in psychoanalysis – a phobia that one is unable to manage life without the lost family member, partner or job. This phobia continues for a long time, giving rise to the second characteristic in psychosynthesis – the lack of hope. This characteristic makes it impossible to make plans for the future, because the individual does not feel good in the present.

These traits, pain and hopelessness, lead to the third element in psychoanalysis – suspicion and the lack of trust in all relationships. The individual begins to doubt everyone. A person with the third characteristic begins to develop a guilty conscious because he cannot open up and express his pain to friends. The individual frets over it and ends up blaming himself for the pain he feels. For example, he does not consider that the partner who left him may be a bad person or that the boss who fired him was at fault - he automatically feels guilty – the guilty conscious being the third fundamental characteristic.

The guilt leads to the fourth element of psychoanalysis - stress and anxiety. Anxiety will lead these people to avoid any kind of confrontation. Say someone does something wrong – like stealing money. Instead of accusing the thief they may even defend them with explanations that make a case for them, for example - he stole because he had no money and needed to eat. They live under the constant stress that someone may disagree or confront them with something. For them everyone except themselves is wonderful and always right. This constant, unnatural stress over having to liberate the rest of the world, affects the person's natural instincts for hunger, thirst and sexual desire (they have sex two or three times a year and can probably eat bread every night for the rest of their lives). This person has now developed the fourth fundamental characteristic of psychosynthesis – the loss of natural instincts. If a person does not have basic instincts (eating, sleeping, sex) then they lack basic conditions for human existence, making them constantly confused. For example, we drink water when we are thirsty, eat food when we are hungry and have sex when we feel aroused. These are the biological similarities in humans and animals. Only after a person has satisfied his basic instincts does he begin to express his feelings and think in scientific and philosophical ways.

When an individual reaches a point where he cannot even concentrate enough to read a book, an article in the newspaper or watch a film on television then he has developed the fifth element in psychosynthesis – constant confusion. The person becomes so confused that he loses basic orientation and withdraws from all human contact into the proverbial small dark room.

A constant pain in the muscles and body develops - this is the sixth element in psychoanalysis and is known as the black zone. The person is now suffering so much that he has no desire to make contact with other people. This is complicated further by other people not understanding this pain and thinking that the depressed person is just being dramatic. The sixth characteristic means that the person does not even dare go outside the door– total and complete seclusion.

When there is nobody this person can rely on, he flees into his own fantasy world, thus developing a hypochondriac or paranoid vision of reality. Because these people suffer so much and have no contact with others, they believe that they have developed diseases such as cancer or are going to have a heart attack. This is the seventh element in psychoanalysis. If these people continue to suffer continuously for between thirty days to three months and are unable to cope then they commit suicide to liberate themselves from this conceptual fantasy world – the seventh and final characteristic.

EPILOGUE

Every client goes through some fundamental, unconscious phases in the therapeutic process. The phases come about progressively while dealing with a symptom - most symptoms go through three different phases. It is essential to keep in mind that different symptoms will develop through these phases differently. For example, an alcoholic's first phase is very different from a marijuana user or manic depressive's first phase. Certain symptoms though – melancholy and martyrs – go through four phases. Depression is the worst since depressive clients develop through five phases, where each phase is a complete metamorphosis. During the process even the client cannot see the transformation - it is recognizable only to us as therapists. Once a client has completed the first phase, he will never go back to that state, because he has now has built another ego or metamorphosis. The first phase of depression is while the client is in the black zone (characterized by pain in the muscles and entire body, isolation from the outside world for up to forty days and constant crying). When the client comes out of the black zone, he will move on to the second phase and never return to first. More specifically he releases himself from his pain and displays traits of the second phase - a new ego, like a happy little five-year child.

I, like any other mental health professional, can easily classify the hundreds of depressed clients (endogenous depression) clients I've had into two categories. The first category is clients who are in therapy for the first time and the second and most common category is the clients who have been in therapy with other therapists or psychologists.

The second category can be divided into three subgroups (below) and it is interesting to note that I have never met a single client within the second category who had completed the first phase with another therapist. It was just not possible to establish even simple dialogue so as a natural consequence they continue to live in the 'black zone' (deep depression):

1. Depressed people aged 40-55 years

Although these people have been in and out of psychiatric counseling in periods as long as twenty or thirty years, have taken plenty of antidepressants, and even tried different forms of therapy like psychodynamic and cognitive therapy, none of them who have ever completed the first phase. All are in the black zone and are therefore deeply depressed. 50% of these people have completes all five phases, freed themselves and built a new ego through the Sisifos method. When I check up on these people 10-15 years after therapy, they are happy and have built a new life without a relapse into depression. Another 30% of this group completed three phases, so they are not depressed anymore but still fear life. This means that they cannot build a new life, get a new job but at least continue without guilt and self-inflicted torture. The remaining 20% completed two phases, which means that they go about life in a childish manner, making innocent remarks and asking naive questions, but with pleasure and without guilt.

2. Depressed people aged 30-45 years

70% of this sub-group completed all five phases. 20% completed four phases, which means that they can build a family and get a job if they want to but not both. 10% completed three phases, which means that they complain periodically to express their aggression towards friends or family. But they can play a role in their family, listen to and protect their children, but find it very difficult to express love, which is always through half-hearted attempts.

3. Depressed people aged 16-30 years

This sub-group never experiences the full 'black zone' (physical pain in the entire body). They cry because they feel guilty and are lonely, but have social skills and can communicate with other people up to a certain level. When they have finished high school they cannot complete a higher education, if they start one it is usually abandoned after 2 years. Their episodic depression is what is known as the 'grey zone'. 80% of this sub-group completed all five phases. 15% completed four phases and only

5% completed three phases. These last 5% cannot cope with solid work and therefore work in periods, but they are able to build a family and have children. They cannot see the complete realities of life and often lapse into fantasy about being artists.

The five transition phases or metamorphoses are the theme and explained in greater detailed in another book, which is the second part of this trilogy about depression. There you will, as a therapist, be surprised to read about the apparent transformation in clients - especially the changes that come about between the second and third phase. If you are not prepared, you may be quite shocked – you'll see sweet, innocent child-like adults change into something totally unexpected and frightening.

As I have described in this book, clients display the same reaction patterns in the five transition phases of the therapeutic process. This means that they cannot go straight from the first phase to the fourth, but instead the phases are incremental and progressive. In other words a depressed client must go through five specific phases or metamorphoses in order to achieve liberation and build a new ego.

The same treatment results are applicable to the first category of depressed people - those who come into therapy for the very first time. It is very clear that the client's age is a major factor. So, if a client is between 45 and 50 years, we can expect that he only has a 50% chance of completing all five phases, etc.

From when I first developed the Sisifos method in 1992 up until now; I have not changed it because it gives effective results and truly works. But for a psychologist to be able to work with the Sisifos method, besides the necessary psychological insight, it is necessary to establish natural boundaries (without scolding or scaring) and to truly care for the client. You can read more in another of my books about which kind of people and what it takes to be a successful therapist.

This first book aims simply to establish some basic fundamentals for working with the Sisifos method. I also intend that this book awakens an interest and desire in the other psychological schools or therapists who go to 'war' in the battle against depression and then give up and call it 'an inherent symptom', as is often done. I am by no means finished with talking about depression, because we still need to solve many mysteries, one of them being why fully half of all clients do not complete all five phases of the therapeutic process.

Sas eftharisto